Richard Francis Weymouth

On early English Pronunciation

With especial Reference to Chaucer

Richard Francis Weymouth

On early English Pronunciation
With especial Reference to Chaucer

ISBN/EAN: 9783337063153

Printed in Europe, USA, Canada, Australia, Japan

Cover: Foto ©ninafisch / pixelio.de

More available books at **www.hansebooks.com**

ON

EARLY ENGLISH PRONUNCIATION,

With especial Reference to Chaucer,

IN OPPOSITION TO THE VIEWS MAINTAINED BY

MR. A. J. ELLIS, F.R.S.,

IN HIS WORK

"ON EARLY ENGLISH PRONUNCIATION, WITH ESPECIAL REFERENCE
TO SHAKSPERE AND CHAUCER."

BY

RICHARD FRANCIS WEYMOUTH, D.Lit., M.A.,

FELLOW OF UNIVERSITY COLLEGE, LONDON.

PREFACE.

It is now nearly four years since I first laid lance in rest to tilt at Mr. Ellis's views—expounded in a work of already 996 closely printed pages 8vo., and still growing—by reading before the Philological Society a paper in opposition to them. How I waited year after year, hoping, in the case of a book which cannot but have an exceedingly limited sale, that the expense would be at least partly borne by the Society of which I have been a member for nearly a quarter of a century, and how the hope has proved to be vain, boots not to tell. Suffice to say the delay has enabled me to avail myself of the few and scanty intervals of leisure that relieve an engrossing and harassing profession, to enlarge and to a great extent rewrite the paper, though it still is far from being as complete as I could wish. But I have no time to enlarge yet further, and must therefore console myself with the reflection that at least in some people's estimation a great book is a great evil, and that an argument, if sound, is often none the worse for being condensed.   R. F. W.

Mill Hill School, Middlesex, N.W.
April, 1874.

TABLE OF CONTENTS.

Section		Page
1.	Introductory	1
2.	Our starting point must be *spoken*, not written, language . .	1
3.	Mr. Ellis's delusive maxim that "the orthography shows the sound"	2
4.	Orthoepists not to be too much relied on	2
5.	Their statements how used by Mr. Ellis	4
6.	Traditional pronunciation our main guide	5
7.	In dealing with other languages Mr. Ellis unhesitatingly admits the evidence of traditional pronunciation . . .	6
8.	The separate dialects so many separate witnesses . . .	6
9.	See for example the permanence of the characteristic peculiarities of the Scottish dialect	7
10.	No reason to believe that civil war has greatly changed our spoken language	9
11.	Nor foreign invasion	10
12.	Other sources of information	10
13.	As to I (ɔi) words, Dutch and German confirm the evidence of our own dialects : list of words	11
14.	By aid of these words others may be determined . . .	13
15.	This positive evidence not to be flung aside the moment an objection appears	13
16.	An objection based on Palsgrave's expressions . . .	14
17.	Further evidence that *i* final was (ɔi) in French . .	14
18.	Confirmed by many Dutch words of French derivation . .	16
19.	Salesbury's statements as to I words . . .	16
20.	True theory as to these (ɔi) words	16
21.	The sound of (ɔi) sometimes written *ei* in English as well as in German	17
22.	The English pronunciation of the Latin *i* defended by Lipsius .	18
23.	A ray of light from an old inscription in Æolic Greek . .	18
24.	Conclusion, for the present, as to I words. (See below, § 109) .	19
25.	Fresh objections brought by Mr. J. A. H. Murray from the Scottish mode of writing Celtic proper names . .	19
26.	No such evidence derivable from Welsh . .	20
27.	OU words . . .	21
28.	The vowels in their natural sequence . .	21

TABLE OF CONTENTS.

Section		Page
29.	Nature of diphthongs, which are not simply two vowels combined	22
30.	Definition of diphthong	23
31.	Applied to English *ou*, German *au*, Dutch *ui*, &c. . .	23
32.	Traditional evidence as to OU words	24
33.	Confirmed by German and Dutch, just as that about (əi) words: list	25
34.	*Roun, douve, doust, úp, us*	25
35.	Objection from Palsgrave	26
36.	Words in *ou* of French derivation were sounded with (əuu) .	26
37.	Second objection from Chaucer, and the Cuckoo Song .	27
38.	*Cuckow* and *prow* imperfect imitations of the French originals .	28
39.	Negative arguments: first, other words contain (uu), and will not rhyme with *ou* words	28
40.	Second, orthoepists do not make our *ou* = Italian *u* .	29
41.	Third, Cheke and Smith's account of *ov* . . .	29
42.	Fourth, Smith's (uu) words not written *ou* . . .	29
43.	Fifth, other grammarians always distinguish (uu) and (əu) words precisely as in modern English	30
44.	In a few exceptional words *ou* was = (u) or (uu) . .	30
45.	Disuse of Anglo-Saxon accents: the spoken words still distinguished	31
46.	The Anglo-Saxon *á* became O	32
47.	Apparent exceptions really Old Norse words, not Anglo-Saxon; only observe	33
48.	Mr. Murray's view of the Scandinavian element in the Northern dialects	33
49.	The (o) sound confirmed by French and Italian . .	34
50.	(Chaucer's *gat-toothed*)	34
51.	Anglo-Saxon words in *ó* had the sound of (uu) modern English OO	35
52.	Their Dutch and German congeners confirm this . .	36
53.	(*Did* not a reduplicate preterit)	37
54.	Words in *á* in Anglo-Saxon, and those with *ó*, written alike in Chaucer's time, but demonstrably not pronounced alike .	38
55.	Occasional exceptions mistaken by Mr. Ellis for the rule .	40
56.	Recapitulation on O words	41
57.	*Could, would, should*	41
58.	The symbols AI and EI sounded as in modern French .	42
59.	As proved from the Old Norse and Old French originals of certain of these words	43
60.	Whence others in (æd), (æth), (æn) may be determined, many of them with distinct and separate evidence from Old Norse, Old French, Old Dutch, &c.	44
61.	In like manner, the authority of Meigret and the assonances of the Chanson de Roland, &c., fix *eis* and *eit* . .	44
62.	Three exceptions in French: Palsgrave on *ai* . .	45
63.	No exceptions in Chaucer, where *ai* words rhyme with one another without distinction	46

TABLE OF CONTENTS. ix

Section		Page
64.	And etymology, assonances, &c., show the sound to have been (ee)	46
65.	Palsgrave again on *ai*	47
66.	Many of these *ai* words may have had an older sound (*ai*)	47
67.	Summary of arguments as to *ai* words	48
68.	A words: Chaucer's *a* certainly not (æ), but some (a) sound	49
69.	The change of *a* from (a) to (æ) earlier in Scotland than in England, and undoubtedly aided by Old Norse	49
70.	Yet it is not through Stuart influence that the change took place in England	50
71.	A had in many words even in Queen Elizabeth's time a sound intermediate between (a) and (ee)	51
72.	Classes of *a* words in Chaucer: some had (a);	52
73.	Others (A)	52
74.	A third class short (æ)	53
75.	A fourth a longer (æ) or (aæ) Ormin's *å*	54
76.	A *w* preceding did not give the sound of (A)	56
77.	Mr. Ellis supposes Chaucer's *a* to have been always (a)	56
78.	Tradition fixed the sound in a large number of E words as (ii); Anglo-Saxon mode of writing, *é*	57
79.	Pronunciation of *ai* and *ó* in Anglo-Saxon. (See also §§ 107, 108.)	58
80.	Derivation of *she*	58
81.	The broad sound of *e* as (æ) in the Western dialects only partial: the line drawn	59
82.	Dutch and German congeners of many of our *e* words also have (ii)	60
83.	Or a sound near (ii), as had also certain of these words in other languages	60
84.	Words spelt at a later time with EA had some (e) sound: they never rhymed with EE words	61
85.	Nor did these classes of words rhyme in Chaucer, although not distinguished in spelling	63
86.	Final *e* in Chaucer was (ii)	63
87.	*Parde*	64
88.	Tendency to Anglicize foreign words	64
89.	Latin no exception: a traditional pronunciation of ecclesiastical Latin has no existence	65
90.	French words in final (ai), (eə), and (é) adopted into English, and Anglicized, the third becoming (ii) or (*i*), as all three classes are sounded now	66
91.	Words ending in *-ere* not all pronounced alike: some had (ii) like modern *here*, some (ee), like *there*: the two classes quite distinct	66
92.	French words in *-ier* or *-iere* belong to the (ii) class. (Footnote on the genuineness of two lines bracketed by Mr. Wright in his edition of the Cant. Ta.)	68
93.	Pronunciation and meaning of Chaucer's name	69
94.	Influence of final *e* in words that in French ended in *-iere*	70
95.	Words in *-ene* also in two distinct classes	70

TABLE OF CONTENTS.

Section		Page
96.	As also in -*eme*	71
97.	And in -*eke*	71
98.	And in -*ale*, with one or two troublesome exceptions	72
99.	And in -*ete*	72
100.	In the former of all these pairs of classes the sound was (ii)	73
101.	In the second class of each of these pairs the vowel was not (ee) or (eei), except only in certain words in -*ete*	73
102.	Can the sound have been (æa)?	74
103.	Objections to this view. (Footnote on Milton's and Dryden's rhymes)	74
104.	True sound that of (ee)	75
105.	This view confirmed by modern pronunciation	75
106.	The distinction between the two classes of *e* words equally marked in Anglo-Saxon	76
107.	The exact value of *eó* in Anglo-Saxon ;	76
108.	And of *eá*	77
109.	Final argument on I words	78
110.	Supposed *tendency* to change (ii) words into (əi)	79
111.	Another view suggested as to the use of the written *i* or *I*	80
112.	Last words about (əu)	83
113.	Is *ai* properly the symbol for (a) + (i) ?	84
114.	Two classes of *ei* words in Old High German	85
115.	The short *e* in Chaucer was (e)	85
116.	Did the Anglo-Saxon *æ* stand for (æa)?	86
117.	Five objections : true sound (ee) ;	86
118.	Which coincides with results already reached	88
119.	The sound represented by AW or AU was (AA) as at present	88
120.	Gil's authority not adverse. (Footnote on Gil's pronunciation)	88
121.	Bullokar, Hart, Smith, Salesbury, and Palsgrave, on *au*	90
122.	Short (æ), short (e), short (i), represented in Anglo-Saxon by *a*, *e*, and *i*. (Footnote on Professor Hadley's paper on English Vowel Quantity)	92
123.	Short *a* in Anglo-Saxon was (a)	93
124.	The sounds of *æ* and *e* very near each other ; the two modern pronunciations of *ate*	93
125.	Chaucer's short *e* : *lesse, lasse : lefte, lafte*	93
126.	The final *e* when sounded ?	94
127.	Its sound was not (ii), nor (i)	94
128.	But (e)	94
129.	The short final *e*, in Anglo-Saxon probably (e)	95
130.	*Me, he, thee, we, ye*, in Anglo-Saxon with (e) ; in Early English with (e) ; in both also with (ii)	96
131.	Y probably stood for (y)	97
132.	The short O in Anglo-Saxon and in Chaucer. (See also pp. 122, 123.)	98
133.	The quasi-diphthongal U found only in French words	98
134.	The French *u* had formerly a diphthongal sound	99

Section		Page
135.	And compounded of the same elements as our long *u* (juu) or (iu)	100
136.	Mr. Ellis's transliterations	101
137.	Objection to *u* = (juu) from Cheke and Smith . .	101
138.	The true sound of *u* in French and Scottish was (jyy) .	102
139.	Two classes of EW words according to Palsgrave . .	102
140.	There are, in fact, in Chaucer three such classes: table exhibiting them	103
141.	Class I. of French origin	105
142.	Class II. of Anglo-Saxon origin	105
143.	Class III. of Anglo-Saxon origin	106
144.	Pronunciation of *ew* in Class I. with (jyy) . . .	106
145.	Pronunciation of *ew* in Class II. with (eu) . . .	107
146.	Pronunciation of *ew* in Class III. with (juu) . .	107
147.	Objections from Salesbury	108
148.	Palsgrave's distinctions had died out in the age of Queen Elizabeth: table	110
149.	Another difficulty	110
150.	But is the sound of (ə) of late introduction into our language? Almost identical with (v)	111
151.	Evidence that it existed in Early English, either written with *u* .	111
152.	Or with *a*	112
153.	Reasons against taking this short *a* as (ɒ) . .	113
154.	In Anglo-Saxon also (v) was found . . .	114
155.	OI words	114
156.	The *o* in OI was probably (u)	115
157.	The true sound probably (u*i*) or (u*e*) . .	116
158.	Conclusion	116

APPENDIX: Specimens 120 117

₊ Throughout this Essay, letters, or occasionally syllables or words, written in () indicate sounds according to Mr. Ellis's carefully and ingeniously constructed system of "palæotype." The *KEY TO PALÆOTYPE*, which will be found on a folding leaf at the end of the volume, gives a very small, but probably sufficient, portion of that system.

ON
EARLY ENGLISH PRONUNCIATION.

1 *Introductory.* IT is by no means an agreeable task to assail the conclusions at which the long and laborious and evidently *con amore* researches of a fellow-student have landed him; and it seems futile to attempt to uproot by this short essay those views which his large and learned book has caused to be so generally received in our Society. But as I have for some years had the subject of the present paper before my mind, and the results at which I have arrived differ entirely from Mr. Ellis's on some leading points, and the careful and candid consideration of his work has only to a very small extent modified my views, in the interests of philological truth I cannot consent to be silent.

It is not a lack of industry with which Mr. Ellis can be charged; but I do impeach his logic, and seriously complain of the general conduct of the argument.

2 *Our starting-point must be spoken, not written, language.* It is impossible that a scholar who has devoted many years to philological study, should really confound even for an instant language proper—that is the *living voice*—with the black marks on white paper which are the mere *symbols* of language; but it is quite possible that in dealing simultaneously with both language and its symbols, he may allow its symbols to occupy too prominent a position before his own mind and in his treatment of the subject.

The question before us should, I apprehend, generally shape itself as follows: *not*, what sound did such or such a symbol represent? (though it may conveniently assume that form sometimes); *but, how were such and such spoken* words of this 19th century spoken in the 14th or in the 9th? Mr. Ellis looks always to the symbol.

3 *Mr. Ellis's maxim that "The orthography shows the sound."* Now if we examine in Heywood's Proverbs and Epigrams the rhymes of words ending in *-ear, -eare, -ere, -eere,* and *-eer,* we shall soon find ourselves in inextricable confusion, if the letters alone are to guide us; but if we notice that the words which we now pronounce with (ii)—*cleer, chere, here* (adv.), *here* (vb.), *neere, yeer, deer* (adj.), *deer* (s), and *appeare*—rhyme with one another in Heywood, however he may spell them, but never rhyme with *there, where, were, wear, swear, Edgeware, hair, hare, ear, spear, fear, answer, ere, bear* (vb.), while these all rhyme, most of them repeatedly, with one another; and if examination of Sir Philip Sidney's poems leads (as it does) to precisely the same result, we may be warranted in drawing some conclusion from that fact.

Besides, the former mode of putting the question has a tendency towards the assumption that each symbol, or group of symbols, stood only for one sound, or at most for one pair of sounds, one long and one short. Considering that our first vowel is at present the representative of at least four distinct sounds (as in *fate, fat, father, fall*), and our second vowel of at least three (as in *we, when, were*); we must not assume that it was entirely otherwise five or ten centuries ago. Mr. Ellis leans on the broken reed of the maxim that "The Orthography shows the sound." How untrustworthy the support is—though unhappily we sometimes have no other—will be abundantly proved further on.

But besides trusting far too implicitly to this delusive maxim, Mr. Ellis in conducting his case exhibits singular partiality towards one class of witnesses, while others—by far the most important—he treats with undeserved disrespect: they are not indeed put out of court, but they are by no means allowed full, a patient, and impartial hearing.

4 *Orthoepists not to be too much relied on.* The too highly favoured witnesses are the grammarians and orthoepists, whose evidence may be impugned on the ground, not only that they are often as inaccurate observers as many of us moderns are, and on many points do not agree among themselves, in which respect doubtless their writings only the more exactly reflect the variety of popular usage,* but also that they too commonly are not content to let us know the simple facts—that was not the object they had in view in writing, —but they endeavoured to guide usage to something different from what it was, and too frequently they mislead the modern reader by their assertion that the sound of a word is what it is not: they mean that it is so and so *de jure*, and the reader is apt to think they mean that it is so *de facto*. So Gil charges Hart with seeking rather "ducere quam sequi" our language by his mode of writing; Palsgrave again and again appeals to the speech of those "that pronounce the latine tonge aright," *i.e.* in the manner that *he* approved; Erasmus, Cheke, Smith, all argued from written symbols that a written diphthong must represent a compound sound, and Smith in particular insisted on a distinction between *ai* and *ei* in English, which, though it may have existed in the dialects in certain words, his very insistence, as well as the rhymes of all the poets from Chaucer downwards, show not to have been observed in the received pronunciation; and Butler's language betrays the same tendency where he speaks of a "corrupt" usage. In this last case Mr. Ellis has very justly observed that "allowance must be made for the mode in which orthoepists speak of common pronunciations which differ from their own or from what they recommend—by no means always the same thing" (p. 124); as elsewhere (p. 139) he remarks on Gil's "anxiety to give prominence to the first element" in the diphthong *&c.* All such "anxiety" detracts from the value of a writer's evidence when it is the simple fact that the reader desires to ascertain; and probably many of the sounds which are vindicated by these older orthoepists may deserve to be characterized as "a theoretical pronunciation, which may be as false as that which Erasmus, Smith, and Cheke intro-

---

* Gil says: "In *build* ædificare, nondum iactum est fundamentum; pro suopte enim cuiusque ingenio, vnus *bild* per *i* λεῖον; alter *beeld* per *ei*; tertiu *beeld* per *i* longum; et adhuc quartas *billd* per *i* breue."

duced into England for the Greek language" (see *Academy* for Apr. 15th, 1871). But Mr. Ellis is certainly not unaware of the weakness of his case in this important particular.

There are however other objections to our relying too confidently on these authorities. One is that the earliest of them lived nearly a century and a half after Chaucer. I lay but little stress on this, not believing that any great change took place in the interval. A second is, that these orthoepists—comparative novices in their art—seem to have overlooked sounds which can be shown to have existed in common use in their day. A reader of Ben Johnson's account of *a*, would suppose that that was the symbol for only two sounds, apparently (a) and (A); but Gil twenty years earlier, and Hart seventy, had recognized three classes of words the vowel of which was written with *a*. Smith in his argument about the Greek η points out only two *es* in English, as in *whēt* (wheet), now *wheat*, and *whĕt*; yet he himself in his Index, which Mr. Ellis seems not to have discovered, recognizes another which for our purpose is evidently more important, for he calls it the *e Anglica*, of which *breed* and *heel* are his examples. And so he says elsewhere: " Recte etiam fortasse nunc *Domine ne in furore*, per e Italicum, non quemadmodum olim per illud .e. Anglicum, quod in *bee* cùm apis dicimus, aut *me* cùm ἐμέ nostro more loquamur, obseruatur, &c." De Ling. Gr. Pron., p. 14 v°.

5 *Statements of orthoepists, how used by Mr. Ellis.* But a yet graver objection is furnished by Mr. Ellis's ingenuity, he having shown but too frequently the possibility of extracting from their words a sense totally at variance with what *I* believe they really meant; so that I prefer scarcely to draw any conclusions at all from premises which seem to be so doubtful. For instance—once more to anticipate the general argument— Salesbury represents the English words *true, vertue, duke, Jesu*, by *triw, vertiw, diwk, tsiesiw;* and Mr. Ellis, by a ratiocinative process which I cannot pretend to understand, concludes "that Salesbury's *iw* meant (yy)." I have submitted the words to several educated Welshmen, who all

say that the *u* is (*i*) and the *w* (uu), and the diphthong is as nearly as possible the long English *u*—(iu) or (Juu) of *tune, tube, union*. It seems to me that Salesbury's description implies, in a manner than which nothing can be clearer, that these words were sounded in his time exactly as they are now, except that (trJuu) has become (truu), and the first syllable of *virtue* is no longer sounded (ver).

As to these orthoepists, it must be confessed that their language, as manipulated by Mr. Ellis, is singularly unintelligible; and yet if, instead of studying only fragmentary quotations, and misleading explanations, and "transliterations" which assume every single point that is in dispute, we read the books themselves, and adopt the simple hypothesis that *as a general rule* our forefathers of those centuries pronounced their own language, and Latin and Greek too, just as we do now, almost every difficulty at once disappears.

6 *Traditional pronunciation our main guide.* And who are the witnesses that are thrust aside? *Our dialects as now spoken.*

Suppose we have to inquire concerning certain common and familiar words which we have inherited as part of the old English speech of our forefathers,—for instance, those which we in our 19th century mode pronounce with (ɔi), such as *mine, thine, fine, wine, shine, line, swine, wife, life, knife,* &c. &c.—how these words, as to their strongly accented vowels, were pronounced several centuries ago; I contend that we have above all things to consider how these words are still pronounced in various English dialects—especially of course, for Chaucer, those south of the Humber. It is spoken language about which we are inquiring, and it is mainly language as now spoken that must furnish an answer to our question. The existing English dialects yield by far the most important evidence in the case, and their voice, in this particular part of the inquiry, Mr. Ellis scarcely suffers to be heard. If we listen to them, they with almost perfect unanimity assign to these words some such diphthongal sound as we still give them. There may be some discrepancy in their evidence as to the elements of which the diphthong is composed, but almost all agree that it is certainly not the pure (i), but a diphthong ending in (i).

7   But has it been proved that these witnesses are unworthy of credit? I cannot find the proof. Mr. Ellis has no hesitation in believing—and probably most will agree with him—that those words in which the (i) sound occurs in strongly accented syllables in modern French, Italian, Welsh, modern Greek, &c., preserve in those languages a traditional pronunciation many centuries old; but no reason is assigned for the singular inconsistency of rejecting the like conclusion in a precisely analogous case in the Teutonic languages. Mr. Ellis says confidently (p. 137), when speaking of the sound of the French *eu* in Palsgrave's time, "the reference to Italian *completely establishes* the sound." And again of the same period (p. 149): "There can be no doubt of the Italian *u*, which was certainly (uu)." On p. 164 he speaks in a similar tone of "the real Latin *u* long." Yet elsewhere (p. 530) he lashes "the historical ignorance which assumes that a language may have only one pronunciation through the generations for which it lasts." Now I do not for a moment object to Mr. Ellis's confidence as to the Latin and Italian *u*; but I ask that our English vowels shall be judged on like principles.

In dealing with other languages Mr. Ellis unhesitatingly admits the evidence of traditional pronunciation.

8   Moreover it must not be forgotten that each separate dialect, and even subdialect, is a separate and independent witness. In these days of railways and newspapers and national schools, there are such facilities for locomotion and intercommunication of knowledge and habits of thought and speech, that we find it hard to realize, and are very apt to forget how, even less than a century since, the inhabitants of one rural district were almost completely isolated from their neighbours only ten or twenty miles distant. Very recently I have heard of the death of a villager who during the whole of a long life never once went out of his native parish. And in the Life of Dr. James Hamilton we read:

The separate dialects so many separate witnesses.

"As in all primitive places, the people [of Strathblane] were by no means locomotive. Margaret Freeland for upwards of eighty years never slept under any roof but her own. * * * One man had visited the great metropolis. This venturous spirit .... went by the name of London John." And this too in the beginning of the 19th century. And not only were there no railways. A friend of mine, not yet an octogenarian, tells me that in his childhood the agricultural produce that was brought to Plymouth market was conveyed entirely on pack-saddles and in panniers: wheeled vehicles scarcely existed in the south of Devon, except stage waggons and coaches and the carriages of the wealthy. I may add that my friend's residence as a boy was close to one of the principal gates of the town (long since pulled down), through which much of the traffic would pass. But a rustic population, whether in Devonshire or in Kent, in Norfolk or in Fife, having little or no communication with its neighbours, neither exercising influence upon them nor receiving influence from them, would be certain to maintain its traditional pronunciation, generation after generation, and century after century, as to strongly accented syllables, almost—or altogether—unchanged.

And that this has actually been the case, our early English literature exhibits very numerous proofs. To mention one or two only: Robert of Gloucester's *vever* and *vive* are just as the words are still pronounced in the western counties; the infinitives in *y* in the Southern dialect still exist in Somersetshire, Dorsetshire, and Devonshire;* and the prefixed *a*- as in *ago* was common of old in the South and is common still, rare of old in the North and rare still (for a Scotsman will say "seven years since" or "syne" rather than "seven years ago"). But the Scottish dialect is especially instructive on this point. I will not quote Gawain Douglas nor Sir David Lyndesay, but a poem only about a century younger than the time

9 Permanence of the character in the traditions of the south and the east.

* "Ta raly in the dark es vain." *Nathan H*

of Chaucer—the Lancelot of the Laik edited by Mr. Skeat, the accordance of which with modern Scotch is very striking; for it can be very clearly discerned notwithstanding the party-coloured disguise—half Southern, half Midland—which the dialect wears. As to that accordance, I of course do not refer to the frequent occurrence of *old* forms: that is only what might be expected. But several of the distinctive features of Modern Scotch, such as we find it in Scott's novels or Burns's poems, and which are *departures* from the Anglo-Saxon or Old Norse or Old French originals, we have already in Lancelot of the Laik. Such are the forms *ony* and *mony*; *fecht*; *lap*, as preterit of *leap*; *hard* for *heard*; *ee*, rhyming with *hee*, for *eye*; *tane* and other parts of *take* (from the O.N. *taka*) with the *k* dropped; *our* (i.e. *ou'er*) for *over*; *loe* (or *lo'e*, as Burns writes it) for *love*; preterits and participles in -*it*, as *behovit*, *closit*, *armyt*; the final *t* or *d* dropped, as in *correk'*, *roun'*; the sound of *aw* (AA) or (aa) apparently in *walkin* for *waken* —just as *hawk* is spelt *halk*—in *chalmer* for *chamber* (where the Scots never pronounce the *l*), and in *magre* and *matalent* where a radical *l* is dropped; *ā* for *ē* in *felouschip*, *rapref*, *raquest*, *rakning*, &c.; and in *cercumstans* for *circumstance* and many other words we find *i* changed into *ē*, *aediois*, *revere*, *prekand*, *steropes*, *prevaly*, *deligent*, *fragelitee*, *inequitee*, &c. I may add that Barbour and the "Louthiane Inglis," specimens of which have so recently been edited by Mr. Lumby, exhibit just the same features. But the fact that in minute details such as these the language has remained unchanged for more than four centuries shows with what masoretic accuracy tradition may hand down certain parts of the pronunciation of a dialect through a long period of time. In fact our provincial dialects and sub-dialects constitute a most important body of independent witnesses; and to omit them from consideration is no less absurd than if a mathematician should treat on Statics and omit to consider the force of Gravitation, or an astronomer should discourse on the Solar System and forget the Sun. Mr. Ellis does indeed quote exceptional dialectic pronunciations.

In other words, his Solar System contains comets, but for all that it has no Sun.

But the separate dialects, it is urged, have all been changing simultaneously: there is an inherent tendency to change, not so much in the Celtic and Romance languages, but in all of the Teutonic stock; and Dutch and English, though less in contact with each other than any two English dialects, have run a parallel course. I reply that the dialects of even adjoining counties in England were formerly in a state of mutual isolation almost as complete as the Dutch and English; and that as to this tendency in speech, as in a living, growing, developing organism, while it must be admitted that there is some evidence for it, derived from modes of writing, there are yet very considerable difficulties to be overcome. I will return to this question by and by, after having discussed the *I* and *E* words: see § 102.

10. But Mr. Ellis refers to civil war as likely to have produced a great change in English pronunciation in the 15th century; but he does not explain why the civil war of the 17th century did not produce like important changes: for it is vain to assert that it did. But in fact these Wars of the Roses afford only the merest shadow of an argument in favour of the supposition that owing to them such an expression as "the *fine wine* that *my wife* gave to the *child*" (oi) would thirty years earlier have been "the *feen ween* that *mee weef* gave to the *cheeld*" (ii). So stagnant had the population in its normal condition been, that the marching and countermarching of armies, and here and there probably the remaining behind of a wounded man as an inhabitant of some town or village near the scene of fight, seemed an astounding "commyxstion and mellynge" of the people. But what great effect upon the language of the people would or could be thus produced? Let us look at the case. A hostile army marches through a sparsely-peopled district, or encamps in it for a few weeks, or garrisons a town. What follows? I will not ask whether it is likely that

No reason to believe that civil war has greatly changed our spoken language.

under these unpropitious circumstances the two parties would combine to improvise an Accademia della Crusca for the purpose of devising orthoepical innovations; for I have no wish to parody or caricature Mr. Ellis's opinions: I have too sincere a respect for his philological attainments. But this much his argument seems to me really to imply: that both parties by common consent came somehow no longer to say "feen ween" and "mee weef" (ii), but "fine wine" and "my wife" (əi), adopting, from no cause that can be discovered and with no motive that any ingenuity can divine, a mode of speech equally and utterly unknown to both parties before!

11 *Nor foreign invasion.* Nor will the supposition of foreign influence avail to account for the imagined change. Had it been the case that during the two centuries that intervened between Chaucer and Shakespeare some William of Orange had established himself here, supported by a Dutch Guard some hundred thousand strong, or that Dutch artisans had settled in great numbers as colonists throughout the kingdom, such an event might have been a sufficient cause for the change of *meen weef* into *mine wife* in imitation of the Hollanders (assuming such to have been their pronunciation); but no such event occurred. Nor, as I believe, did any such change in English speech take place.

12 But in addition to the various dialects of English, and besides orthography and the orthoepists, to whose testimony we will now and then lend a cautious ear, other *Other sources of information.* sources of information are—1, the languages cognate to English, especially the Dutch and German; 2, the rhymes and assonances of cognate languages; 3, the derivations of words, to which Mr. Ellis has been singularly indifferent; and 4, the rhymes of our Early English poets, from which (as well as those of later poets) results of great value can be obtained, as will be shown below in at least three important instances, by observing the classes of words which do *not* rhyme though similarly spelt, as well as those that do—a species of negative evidence which has been wholly overlooked by Mr. Ellis, but which of itself suffices to overthrow almost his whole system.

13   So much by way of preliminary observation. And now to enter fairly on our investigation, let us examine first the class of words already alluded to—*mine, fine,* &c., which may for convenience' sake be distinguished as the *I* words. In these our inquiry will be how the strongly accented vowel was formerly pronounced; and, as above remarked, the answer in which all our southern dialects concur is that the sound was (ɔi): they have all preserved traditionally a sound more or less closely approaching, if not identical with, that diphthong: in all there is one or more of the (a) sounds followed by one or more of the (i) sounds, and the pair or series compressed into very nearly the same compound vowel. (On the exact nature of diphthongs see below, § 29.) But we are not left to the voice of English tradition alone; for in a considerable number of those words the root vowel is the same in Dutch and German as in English, the Dutch *ij* and German *ei* both being (ɔi). Here is the list.

As to I *(ɔi) words, Dutch and German confirm the evidence of our own dialects: list of words.*

Engl.	Du.	Germ.
mine	mijn	mein
thine	dijn (Kil.)	dein
fine	fijn	fein
wine	wijn	Wein
shine	schijn	scheinen
line	lijn	Leine
pine (vb.)	pijn (s.)	Pein (s.)
swine	zwijn	Schwein
wife	wijf	Weib
life	lijf	Leibe
knife	knijf (Kil.)	Kneif
drive	drijven	treiben
dike	dijk	Deich
like	gelijk	gleich
bite	bijten	beissen
smite	smijten	schmeissen
thyme	rijm	Reim

(bird) lime	lijm	Leim
slime	slijm	Schleim
ice	ijs	Eis
wise (adj.)	wijs	weise
wise (s.)	wijze	Weise
iron	ijzer	Eisen
mile	mijl	Meile
while	wijl	Weile
pipe	pijp	Pfeife
ripe	rijp	reif
gripe	grijpen	greifen
wide	wijd	weit
ride	rijden	reiten
side	zijde	Seite
tide	tijd	Zeit
glide	glijden	gleiten
idle	ijdel	eitel

To these may be added *riche*, which, though it has the *i* in modern times, is always long in the Ormulum and Chaucer and Early English generally, and is the Du. rijk, Germ. reich.

Inasmuch then as the root vowel in all these words is pronounced alike as (əi) by the Dutch and the High Germans, as well as all the branches of the Engeleyn, while in the same words the vowel is (ii) in certain other Gothic languages (the Scandinavian, for instance, and the Platt-Deutsch), and there is no satisfactory evidence of any change in the pronunciation of these words,* the conclusion seems inevitable that the Angles and Saxons and Hollanders and High Germans constitute a separate division (of course capable of subdivision) of the Teutonic race, and that this sound of (əi) existed in their languages in common at a period prior to the divergence of these tribes from one another. In other words, it seems to me probable that the present vowel sounds of *mine wine* were common to the Englisc, Hollandsch, and Deutsch, from a period of remote antiquity long prior to historical times.

* This point is further discussed in § 102.

14 The sound was written in A.S. *í*, and in E.E. *i, y, ii*, or
ij; and by the aid of rhymes these 35 words
suffice to fix all E.E. words similarly spelt, and
others. Others, thus:* if the pronunciation
of *wide* and *side* can be determined, that of *espide*, which
rhymes with these, is fixed, and therefore that of *espy*. If
we fix *shine* with (ɔi), its preterit in such rhymes as those on
p. 3 of the Allit. Poems—*schynde, kynde, ynde, tynde, grynde,
blynde*—determines these others: a result, I may add, contrary to Mr. Ellis's view (p. 276), but confirmed by Orm's
spelling of *kinde, grindesst,* and *blind;* while elsewhere these
words rhyme with *find*, which Orm spells with the single *n*,
as also we have *findan* with the accent in the Gloucester
Fragments. I am aware that in MSS. the accent on the i
when it stands next to a u, an n, or an m, often serves the
purpose only of the later dot, that is, to show which of the
upright strokes is the vowel. But in the Glouc. Fr. the
writing is so large and clear, and the n is so distinct from
the i, that I believe the accent to be fully intended as such.

<small>By means of
these words
others may be
determined.</small>

15 Whately lays it down as an important rule
in reasoning, that where there exists a body of
positive evidence in favour of any conclusion,
such body of evidence is not to be set aside the
moment we meet with an objection which we do not see
how to surmount. Now we have a mass of such positive
evidence as to the sound of *i* in the words I am discussing,
and to the conclusion to which it leads, I should be prepared to hold even if from imperfect knowledge (for that is
often all that an objection appeals to) I were unable to get
over the difficulty that presents itself from a certain quarter,
and upon which almost exclusively Mr. Ellis fixes his gaze.
I refer to the rhyming of many of our English *i* words with
French words containing the same *written* letter, which it
is affirmed was sounded (*i*). But after all the objection
seems by no means insurmountable; for on turning to
Palsgrave, whose evidence is very "perplexing" to Mr.
Ellis, he states most distinctly (as quite correctly quoted

<small>This positive
evidence not to
be flung aside the
moment an objection appears.</small>

<small>* Compare § 60.</small>

by Mr. Ellis) that the French *i* has two *diverse* sounds, one of them like the Italian *i*, and as we sound *e* in *bee* an insect, *fee* a reward; while as to the second he says, "If *i* be the first letter in a frenche word or the *laste*, he shall, in those two places, be sounded like as we do this letter *y* in these words with vs, *by* and *by*, *a spye*, *a flye*, *awry*, and suche other."

16 *An objection based on Palsgrave's expressions.* Very good, then if any one asserts that these words were sounded (bii and bii), (spii), (flii), (arii), he has Palsgrave dead against him, affirming as Palsgrave does that the *y* here had *not* the sound of the Italian *i*. What sound then had it? The English dialects answer with one voice, declaring first how these words are sounded themselves, and secondly how others are sounded which rhyme with these in Chaucer. First, they declare the words themselves to be sounded with (əi). Secondly, *by and by* rhymes with *why*, with the adverbial termination *-ly* (i.e. *like*, as it is *lijk* in Dutch; and this *-ly* always kept the vowel long till about the middle of the 17th century*); and the single *by*, which is the Dutch *bij* and German *bei*—the very same sound—rhymes with *nigh*, *sky*, and *I* (Dan. *jeg*, pronounced ɹəi). Then *spy* or *aspy* or *espy*, rhymes with *eye*, *high*, *dry*, *I*, *hie*, *sly*, *cry*; and its past tense rhymes with *betide*, *side*, *wide*, *abide*, and these again with *hide*, *chide*, *slide*, *glide*, &c.; and the pronunciation of these the Dutch and German *Tijd*, *Zeit*, *glijden*, *gleiten*, &c., as we have already seen, confirm. Palsgrave's *fly* and *awry* in like manner rhyme with *by* and *aspy* and all the others with which these rhyme. Surely all this evidence is not to be pooh-poohed.

17 *Further evidence that i final was (əi) in French.* And then again as to the sound of *i* as (əi) not (ii) in French, Mr. Ellis himself—whose honesty and candour in argument deserve to be both admired and imitated—mentions a statement made by Mons. Le Héricher that the pronunciation of *joli* as *jolaï* (that is, nearly or quite with our English *i*) is still

---

* Since this sentence was written, our Mill Hill carrier, a Middlesex man, has told me he would do so and so "accordingli" (əi).

known in Normandy, and Dr. Le Taillis of Montebourg near Cherbourg states that this sound is "très-généralement usité" in Montebourg and the neighbourhood. Discredit has been thrown upon these statements because many people have *not* heard these sounds. Just so, when I resided in France in the neighbourhood of Boulogne, one day when a wasp was buzzing in the room, I noticed that my hostess—I was lodging at a village inn—called it "une vêpe;" and I have since, when mentioning the fact, been seriously assured by well-informed Frenchmen that I was mistaken, and that there is no such word in existence. But I heard it. I noticed instantly that it was the Latin *vespa* without the prefixed guttural. To make assurance doubly sure, I got her to repeat the word. And though millions may *not* have heard *vêpe*, I did; and that I should maintain not a whit the less tenaciously, even if I had not recently discovered that my observation is confirmed by Duméril.* The conclusion then to which the testimony of these witnesses conducts us is that what in modern French is enem(i) was in Chaucer's time enem(əi), mere(i), (mere(əi), and Gu(i) Gu(əi); and Chaucer's rhymes show clearly that the final *e* made no difference after this vowel, as *companye, flatterie, curtesye, tyrannye, melodie, contrarye, Lumbardye,* rhyme indifferently with the same words with which *enemy* and *merci* and *Guy* rhyme. From many or most of these modern English fashion has removed the final accent; but that the vowel in Chaucer's time was sounded full and strong, as we still sound it in *glorify, magnify, prophesy, multiply, lullaby,* &c., is clearly evident.

18   And however strange such words may now sound to our ears, this termination is very common in Dutch, as in

* But God forbede but men shulde leve
Wel more thing than men han seen with eye!
Men shal not wenen every thing a lye
But yf himselfe yt seeth, or elles dooth;
For, God wot, thing is never the lasse sooth,
Though every wight ne may it not y-se.
The *Prologe of Nine Goode Wymmen.*
Many have made similar observations since Chaucer's time.

This confirmed by many Dutch words of French derivation. *visscherij, bakkerij, weverij, posterij, olieslagerij, spotternij, jokkernij, schilderij, tooverij, hoovardij, gasterij, voogdij*, &c.; and others there are which are simply French words which seem as if they had been embalmed in Dutch with their antique sound expressly to corroborate Palsgrave's statement which might otherwise seem incredible to us moderns. Such are *Marij, poezij, copij, harpij, galerij, tirannij*, besides others which have a consonant after the vowel, as *Latijn, Martijn* (like the *Austijn* and the *Gamelijn* of, or attributed to, Chaucer), and *patrijs* = perdrix, *prijs* = prix, *paradijs*. I do not lay equal stress on all of these words because of the obvious possibility (I do not admit more) that some of them may have come directly from the Latin.

19 But the majority of grammarians seem to Mr. Ellis to confirm his opinion that the symbol *i* stood for (ii) at least as late as the early part of the 17th century. A few words only on this point.

Salesbury's statements as to 'I' words. Next to Palsgrave comes Salesbury, who, writing for Welsh readers, represents *I, vine, wine* by *ei, vein, wein;* and Mr. Ellis himself admits that "in modern Welsh the sound of *ei* seems to me as (əi)," nor is there a shadow of proof that the Welsh orthography has altered as to the value of *ei* since Salesbury's time. Yet Mr. Ellis immediately after the above admission proceeds with curious inconsistency (p. 111): "I think however that his letters *ei* justify me in considering, or rather leave me no option but to consider, that the English diphthong sounded (ei)* to Salesbury):" words which might with exactly equal force of reasoning be applied to Adelung or Grimm's pronunciation of the modern German *mein* and *wein*.

20 *The true theory as to these (əi) words.* There is surely room for another theory, based not on symbols but on spoken words, as follows: almost universal tradition fixes the words (məin wəin) for many long centuries in the Germanic races; and when the Roman alphabet came to be employed to repre-

* Which Mr. Ellis explains as "Scotch *tine*, Portuguese *ei*."

sent sounds not recognized (I do not say unknown) in the Latin language, at least as then spoken, it came somehow to be customary in this island to represent this sound by *i* or *í*, and among the continental High Germans by *i*, *ii*, or *í*, or at a later time, the Moeso-Goths setting the example, by the digraph *ei*: (see below § 102.) It had to be represented one way or another, and these were the ways adopted. The digraph which the Germans chose stood for another sound (*ee*) in Old French and in the English of Chaucer and his contemporaries, as I shall show below.

(But the accents, it will be said, merely indicated the long vowel. Such is Dr. Bosworth's view: see his Orosius, Pref. p. lxiii. The Teutons borrowed their letters from the Romans, and therefore *a* was (a), *á* (aa), *i* was (i), *í* (ii), and so on. Plausible as this view is, I cannot accept it. The Romans needed no marks of quantity, and made no distinction in writing between *incĭdit* and *incīdit*, *rĕfert* and *rēfert*, *confŭgit* and *confūgit*, and so on; nor therefore did the Teutons learn from them any mode of marking mere quantity. Nor have the moderns found any necessity for so marking the length: is there any book other, or later, than the Ormulum in which indications of quantity are given? And where in Icelandic an accent—or mark, as Rask calls it—is put over a vowel, it in most cases, if not all, indicates a considerable modification of the sound. According to Mr. Ellis, whose accuracy of ear may well be trusted, *a* (a), *á* (aau), *e* (e), *é* (iee), *i* (i) or (ii), *í* (ii), *o* (oo), *ó* (eou), *u* (o), *ú* (uu). In no instance does the accent indicate, according to modern Icelandic pronunciation, a simple prolongation of the vowel.)

21 The sound of (*i* sometimes written *ei* in English as well as in German.) At a later time the great learning and voluminous writings of Erasmus, Lipsius, and others, when they had adopted the *ei*, caused their mode of representing the sound to become familiar to English readers also. Hence we find Hart writing *reid bei* for *ride by*, and Gil writing *ei* for *oculus*, which Smith tells us was sounded like *I* *ego*, and *I* or *aye* *etiam* (Ellis, p. 112). But the modern pronunciation

of *ei* as (əi) in certain words—*either, neither,* and one or two more—is probably due to court influence after the accession of the Hanoverian dynasty.

22. *The English pronunciation of the Latin I defended by Lipsius.* What Smith wrote about *ei*, as quoted by Mr. Ellis on p. 121, concerned the *English ei* (*ee*), which was not by any means what Justus Lipsius (1586) intended—Lipsius was a Dutchman, it will be remembered—when he wrote: "Pronunciant etiam nunc (ita accepi) recte soli pæne omnium Europæorum Britanni: quorum est *Regcina, Ameicus, Veita.* Recte dico, quia non aliud insonuit hæc longa quam EI diphthongum." De recta Pron. Lat. Ling., p. 23. So we had in Lipsius's time—and rightly he affirms—a different pronunciation of *regina,* &c. from almost* all the other nations of Europe; and Gil emphatically declares: "retinebimus antiquum illum et masculinum sonum, atque unà etiam laudem quam Justissimus Lipsus [*sic*] nobis detulit in Reginà, in amicà vitâ, &c." All of this becomes instantly intelligible and lucid on the simple supposition that both the Dutchman and the Englishman spoke of the same sound (əi) that tradition has handed down to us.

I have not found in Lipsius's writings any statement of the reasons on which his opinion is based, but they were probably such as these: 1st, that the traditional sound in certain localities was (əi), (see quotation from Sir Thomas Smith in footnote); 2nd, that Greek words with ει generally have the simple *i* in Latin; and 3rd,—for which however in many cases itacism will sufficiently account—that Latin words in *i* are not infrequently found in Greek with ει, as Ἡεῖσαι, Ὠστεία, Λείγηρ, Σειρῖτις.

23. *A ray of light from ancient Greece.* But all southern Europe, it may be said, is against Lipsius. It unanimously affirms that

---

* Could the Lombards have been an exception? Sir Thomas Smith writes: "Quis Anglus Gallum Latinè loquentem, nisi assuetus intelliget? certe ego non potui: at Italum statim, quia nos ab Italis cùm Latinè sonamus, nisi in valde paucis, a Longobardis autem Italiæ propemodum in nulla re dissidemus: at à Gallis infinitum quantum dissentimus, quamvis nostri sint vicini." De Ling. Gr. Pron. (1568), p. 14. I must leave this nut for some student of early Italian pronunciation to crack.

the juice of the grape—to take one typical example—was not called (woin) but (wiin) in the ancient Classical Languages. No doubt it is easy to assume that the Italians, Spaniards, Portuguese, &c., have preserved the true Latin sound of this word; but what of Greek? Some scholars believe that in the οι of οἶνος the ο is merely a variant of the digamma, and that Ϝινος is the old form and points to (wiin). But ancient inscriptions show us the Ϝ and the ο both used in such words. In Bœckh's Corp. Inscr. Gr., No. 4, we have TAN ϜOIKIAN: which, being confirmed also by other inscriptions, conclusively shows that in that word at least—very probably therefore in others like it—the Ϝ was not followed by the pure sound of (ii).

24 *Conclusion as to 'I' words.* And such is the conclusion at which I arrive,* from the evidence of Palsgrave and Mons. Le Héricher, of Salesbury and Lipsius, from that of modern High German and Dutch, and above all from that of our southern English dialects, both literary and provincial; that Chaucer pronounced the class of words which we have been discussing with precisely the same long *i* (ɔi) as we now give to most of them; and that in Southern Anglo-Saxon "the long *i* with an accent, as in *wín, wíf, tím, rím*, was," as Mr. E. A. Freeman has affirmed in the preface to his recently published work,† "*certainly* sounded as it is now."

25 Mr. J. A. H. Murray has called my attention to two facts of considerable importance in reference to Northern English. The first is that all Gaelic proper names that contain (ii) are written with *y* or *i* in Lowland Scottish, in

---

* There is yet one argument which I defer till after discussing some of the Ϝ words : see § 101.

† Old English History for Children, p. xvii. It is pleasant to be able to quote the name of any scholar who is a brother barbarian, if the system of pronunciation for which I contend is indeed so "barbarous" as Mr. Sweet pronounces it in the *Academy* for Oct. 22nd, 1870, p. 27. Whether (wiin) which should be a correct and classical pronunciation now in the mouths of a hundred millions of mankind, and yet deserve to be stigmatized as "barbarous," supposing it to have been used by their ancestors five or ten centuries ago, is not easy to discern. But the question is not to be settled by ...

which they are *now* pronounced with (ɔi). Thus *Cantire* or *Kintyre*, with (ɔi), is Ceanntìr (Kaa'ntiir) in Gaelic, *Fife* is Fìbh (fiiv), *Skye* is Sgiath (skjiiv), *Dalry* is *Dailrighe* (daljriij), and so on. The second is that numerous words with *i* that have been borrowed from Lowland Scottish into Gaelic are pronounced with (ii), as trìabh (triiv) = tribe, prìom (priim) = prime, spìorad (spiiradt) = spirit, prìs (priisj, priish) = price, Crìosd (Kriisdt) = Christ, sgrìobh (skriiv) = write, fìon (fiin) = wine, lìon (liin) = flax, disinn (diisinj, diishinj) = dicing, rìdir (riitjer, riitsher) = eques, mìle (miilə) = mile, tìm (tiim) = time, pìan (piin) = O. E. pyne, pìob (piip) = pipe, and ìarunn (ii-rən) = iron. These facts constitute a double argument which seems to me incontrovertible. It concerns however Northern English only, that is to say the dialects from the Humber to the Moray Frith, whose affinity with Old Norse, and partial derivation from it, quite prepare us to expect (ii) where the southern dialects had (ɔi).

26   But Welsh, it may be said, is the language of a people adjacent not to the Northern but the Southern English, <small>No such evidence derivable from Welsh.</small> and there are instances of Welsh words which when transferred to English underwent just the same change as *Cantire*, the original sound having been with (ii). A good example is *ap Rhys*, which has yielded us the proper names *Rice*, *Price*, and *Brice*. We know that the original sound was, as it still is in Welsh, (riis); and therefore these names were at first (priis) &c.: the English *i*, so it is argued, stood for (ii). But there is not the slightest difficulty in dealing with such cases. A Welshman bearing the name of *Rhys* or *ap Rhys* migrates into England, and spelling his name as hitherto with a *y* or an *i*, still calls himself (riis) or (apriis), and doubtless endeavours to get his neighbours to follow his example; but the name being similar to the familiar *rys* or *prys*, they pronounce accordingly, and he becomes, in spite of himself, (rəis) or (prəis). Another Welshman of the same name, anxious to maintain the sound, changes the spelling, and calling himself *Rees* or *Reece* succeeds in making his neighbours sound the name to his satisfaction. An instance just parallel to this is *crape* from the French *crêpe*: the sound could not have been maintained without a change of the spelling.

The Welsh pronunciation of borrowed words affords no trustworthy evidence, the forms being so much altered. It would for instance be very hazardous to conclude from the Welsh forms *Lundain*, *Ffrainc*, and *Tain*, that the words then first borrowed into Welsh had such sounds as our neighbours give them now: that *London* was (l*i*ndain), *France* (fraink), and *Thames* (tain).

27 'ou' words.   I pass on to the consideration of another compound sound, as to which again our Southern dialects maintain a nearly uniform tradition, namely, the diphthong (so-called) heard in *house*, *mouse*, *ground*, &c. Our dialects do not all give quite the same sound, but in all it is a compound, and made up of nearly the same elements. It may not be amiss to investigate those elements; for though the nature of diphthongs and other compound vowel sounds has been abundantly discussed, the subject is perhaps not yet quite exhausted.

28 The vowels in their natural sequence.   It has been proved by Willis's experiments[*] that the vowels in their natural sequence are

(ii) (ee) (aa) (AA) (oo) (uu);

and this is the truth apparently, but not the whole truth. There are in fact—as is nowhere perhaps more fully shown than in Mr. Ellis's Key to Palaeotype (Early English Pronunciation, pp. 3–10)—numerous, or rather innumerable, intermediate sounds, all delicately shading off into those next to them, that occupy the intervals between these sounds, or extend beyond the series at either extremity. For sounds not used by one nation or in one dialect are familiar in another, not to mention that probably no two individuals who speak any language utter vowels abso-

---

[*] It is rather surprising that Mr. Melville Bell, when propounding his own ingenious observations and complicated vowel system, has not shown the relation of his system to Willis's. The facts which the latter observed and described are still facts, and should not have been ignored. Legions of his overlooked them.

lutely identical, even when these are intended and supposed to be so. By way of illustration, here are a few of these additions to the vowel-scale. At one extremity of the series we have the French (ii) somewhat thinner than our English (ii), and at the other the French *u* and German *ü* (yy) considerably thinner than our (uu). Then between (ii) and (ee) we have (*ii*), or more commonly (*i*) short—which in some dialects, especially in the West of England and north of the Tweed, is apt to approach very near (*e*)—and (*ee*). Between (ee) and (aa) we have (ææ), or more commonly (æ) short, as well as (ɶ) and (ɔ)—these two almost identical. Between (aa) and (AA), with various nuances of sound, we have the Prussian (*aa*). Between (AA) and (oo) there is perhaps no recognized sound intervening. Between (oo) and (uu) we have (*oo*), and the German *ö*, French *eu*, (œ).

This somewhat more complete series may now be seen in the vowels of the following words:—

il (Fr.), *eel, ill, male, mare, man, vau* (Fr.), *bun, path, mann* (Pruss.), *lawn, robe* (Fr.), *robe, jeune* (Fr.), *pool, flûte* (Fr.)

29 Nature of diphthongs, which are not merely two vowels combined. And now I have to observe that in the so-called diphthongs we do not merely sound certain two vowels of this series in immediate juxtaposition, but we *glide* from one to the other, thus of necessity passing with extreme rapidity through all the intervening sounds. A diphthong therefore is not merely two vowels compressed, but a whole series compressed; and it is the length of the series compressed which marks out the diphthongs, and compels us to recognize them as such. When for instance Mr. Melville Bell says, "The diphthongal quality of the English *ā* will not at first be admitted by every reader"—and a similar remark might be made about our *ō**—wherein consists the difficulty of

---

* "It is well known that nearly all the English long vowels, so called, are composed of two distinct elements; in other words, they are diphthongs. For the gratification of those who may wish to know how the Greeks express them in Romaic letters, we give the following table.

ā is sounded nearly like *ü*, *ia* as *fate*, φϊιτ; fare, φιαρ
ĕ ,, ,, ,, *ia, ia* ,, there, τίαρ; mere, μίαρ
ī ,, ,, ,, *äi, äia* ,, spite, σπάϊτ; fire, φάϊαρ

recognizing the diphthongal sound? Simply it escapes observation through the shortness of the series compressed, (*ee*) being united with its near neighbour (ii), and (*oo*) with (uu). But in each of the three diphthongs *ī* (ɔi), *ou* (ɔu), and *oi* (ɔi)—as sounded in *by*, *bough*, *boy*—a long series is compressed into the resultant compound vowel. The long English *u*, which is commonly spoken of as a diphthong —and in this essay I shall for convenience' sake still so call it—is not strictly a diphthong in the same sense; for it does not really consist of (ii) and (uu), but of the semi-vowel* *y* (ɹ) and (uu), and has no more claim to the name of diphthong than has the precisely analogous compound of the semi-vowel (w) and (ii) which we have in the pronoun *we* and the French *oui*.

30 Definition of diphthong.   A diphthong then is a series of vowel sounds taken in their natural order and uttered with extreme brevity and compression; and the differences that exist between the modes in which they are pronounced in different dialects or by different individuals depend on the exact points at which the speaker takes up, and drops, the series. Thus to sound the English long *i* we pronounce one of the (a) sounds and rapidly glide from it into one of the (i) sounds, in the inverse order of the above series; but one speaker will begin with the Prussian (*a*), another with (a), another—and this I think the most usual—with (æ), another nearly with (e); and one will finish with (*i*), which is most common, another with (i), a third—a foreigner probably—with the thin French (i).

31 Definition applied to English *ou*, German *au*, Dutch *u*, &c.   And what of our *ow* or *ou* of *how* and *house*? It clearly begins early in the vowel series, and ends with one of the (o) or (u) sounds: in fact

"ō is sounded nearly like *oer*, *ou* „ *note*, *roert*; *store*, στέω
  ū   „   „   *ior*, *iora* „ *mute*, *moert*; *pare*, πιέται

It will be observed that *i* as in *fire*, and *u* as in *pure*, are each composed of three distinct elements." E. A. Sophocles, Romaic Grammar, p. 3.

* I have discussed elsewhere the nature of the semi-vowels (of which I contend that we have three in English *y*, the *w* of *went*, and *wh*, as well as the true definitions of the terms vowel and consonant. See paper "On the Letter R" in the Transactions of the Philological Society for 1873, pp. 205 to 267.

almost all our vowels are compressed into it. An Essex man speaking of his *house* or *cow* begins his diphthong with (e); the Londoner commonly starts from (æ); while the customary pronunciation begins with (or about) the (ɒ). The *terminus ad quem* is in Essex and commonly (o); but the Devonshire dialect prefers to terminate with (œ): you cannot without an effort advance as far as (u).

In German there is a similar diphthong, differently pronounced indeed—as might be expected—in different parts of Germany. It begins however with (a) or (*a*), and ends with (u) rather than (o). Yet it requires close observation to distinguish the German *Haus* from our *house*. (In Icelandic there is a like diphthong, written *á*, which Mr. Hjaltalín told me was pronounced exactly like the customary English *ow* of *how* and *now*; but see Ellis, p. 540.) And in Dutch we have the well-known *ui* or *uy*, which Mr. Ellis writes in palæotype (ɔy). He adds in a note (p. 235): "In the actual Dutch pronunciation of *huis*, *muis*, it is very difficult to distinguish the sound from (ɔu), and the difference seems mainly produced by altering the form of the lips into that for (yy), which is slightly flatter than for (uu), rather than by bringing the tongue into the (i) position. Still (ɔy) was the best analysis I was able to make on hearing the sound." This my own very careful observation corroborates.

32 To return now to my argument: just as I have above
<small>Traditional evidence as to "OU" words.</small> insisted on the traditional evidence concerning (ɔi), so I argue as to (ɔu). In a certain small class of words a sound almost identical is given in all our southern dialects, having been handed down from generation to generation; and this uniform tradition furnishes evidence of the greatest possible weight, and, unless there be strong opposing evidence, it fixes approximately the ancient sound, whether the symbol be *ou* or *ow*, or, as in A.S., *ú*.

33 Moreover to confirm this evidence, just as in the case of the (ɔi) words, we have in German and Dutch almost the same sound in many of these words; and these too are all monosyllables, in which therefore the stress of the voice rests on this sound so as to render any change of vowel—especially in so many languages and dialects simultaneously—all the more difficult.

This evidence confirmed by German and Dutch, just as that about (ɔi) words: list.

The natural conclusion is that these words had the (ɔu) sound long prior to historical times, and when the great divisions of the Teutonic race had not yet split asunder.

It is needless to give all the dialectic forms, but here is a short list of words in which English, German, and Dutch; all give very nearly the same sound of (ɔu). Of course, if these are fixed, many others that habitually rhyme with them are fixed also, as well as many of the derivatives—

Engl.	Du.	Germ.
house	huis	Haus
louse	luis	Laus
mouse	muis	Maus
loud	luid	laut
owl	uil	——
foul	vuil	faul
howl	huilen	——
brown	bruin	braun
town	tuin (= fence)	Zaun (= fence)
crown (of the head)	Kruin	——
down (= hill)	duin	——
out	uit	aus
sprout	spruit	——
spout	spuit	——
south	zuid	——
sow	——	Sau
bow (vb.)	buigen	——

34 Roun, dowse, doust, up, &c.

And the German *raunen* is very like the old English *roun* whisper, Anglo-Saxon *rún*. To these must be added three others which are now pronounced with the *ŭ* of *but*, namely, *dove*, *dust*, and *up*. The provincial and Early English *dowse* or *dowf* is well known, and in Devonshire *doust* is commonly used in the sense of chaff; the former of these is Dutch *duif*, German *Taube*, and the latter, Dutch *duist*, but not found in German. I know no tradition of *up* sounded as *oup*, but the German *auf* points in that direction, and the Anglo-Saxon word is often found accented (úp). Just so Chaucer's form *ous* for *us* becomes intelligible now by means of the Anglo-Saxon *ús*.

35 *Objection from Palsgrave.* But there are two or three objections to look at. First, Palsgrave speaks of *cowe, mowe, sowe,* as sounded almost like the Italian *u* and the French *ou;* and Mr. Ellis asserts that we *certainly* know what sound these symbols represent. But without insisting on the *un*certainty of this knowledge, and that there may be much meaning in that "almost;" I would urge that both Salesbury and Sir Thomas Smith were nearly contemporary with Palsgrave, the former of whom seems to have known no other word spelt with -*owe* and pronounced (uu) but the word *wowe* (= woo); and the latter expressly makes the nouns *mow* and *sow* (moou) and (soou). I am in the dark as to Palsgrave's meaning. Only I would observe that certainly in Old French, possibly therefore in Palsgrave's time, the symbols *o, u, ou,* &c., at least before *n,* had not the same sound as now. Thus words like *baron, raison,* which in the Chanson de Roland are spelt with *un* or *on,* are rarely assonant with other *u* words, never with other *o* words: they for the most part stand by themselves. It is therefore not unlikely that the sound struck the English ear as approximating to our -*oun*.

36 I have said *approximating,* but the approximation was probably somewhat close. Two reasons lead to this conclusion. *Words in -on of French derivation were sounded with (oun).* First, in Chaucer the English representatives of French words in -*on,* habitually rhyme with *doun, toun, soune, broun, goun,* &c., (doubtless having ceased* to be sounded "somethyng in the noose," as Palsgrave would say); while they scarcely ever rhyme with words in (oon)—as now

---

* I say "ceased" on the supposition that this *anuswoire*, which exists also in modern Welsh, is correctly regarded as among the Celtic, and therefore the earliest, elements of French.

pronounced,—and never, so far as I have observed, with words in (uun).* Secondly, many—indeed I believe all—of the older English derivatives of French words containing *on* have now the sound of (ɔun), as *abound, fountain, mountain*, to *mount*, to *found, confound, profound, noun, renown, renounce, pronounce, announce, round*, and the vulgar *Mounseer* for *Monsieur;* there being very few, if any, exceptions to this rule except where the final unaccented *-oun* has shrunk and withered into (ʊn), as in *mention, nation, extension. Balloon* and *caissoon* are but modern words. It thus becomes an almost necessary conclusion that if the original French words were not sounded exactly with (ɔun), at any rate—for this is the point we are seeking to ascertain—their descendants in English were so sounded.

37 Second objection from Chaucer and the Cuckoo Song. Then there is Chaucer's rhyme of *cuckow* with *how, swow, now*, and *thou*, while it does not rhyme with words like *do*, like *go*, or like *know;* as in the Cuckoo Song also the same word, spelt *cucu*, rhymes with *cu* and *nu;* the forms *cow* and *now* not having yet come into fashion. From these rhymes my conclusion is simply this, that Chaucer and the writer of the Cuckoo Song pronounced the word with (ɔu). But *cuckoo*, it is urged, is an imitative word, and the final vowel is (uu), not (ɔu). True, but if we insist on the natural sound as (uu), how are we to account for the Greek κόκκυξ and κόκκυ? Were not these in all probability sounded not with (uu), but (yy), and later (ii)? And is it really the case in our or in any language that the imitative words are exact imitations? What then of our *neigh, bellow, cackle, laugh*, the Dutch *brieschen, hoest*, the French *rire, tousser, glousser*, &c. &c.? To say that they were once correctly imitative words in an earlier stage of their existence is to say nothing; for Chaucer's *cuckow* was not in its earliest stage, and might as easily appear in a corrupt form as our now familiar *laugh*.

38 Let us look however at the derivation of *cuckoo*. It is

* *Alone, bone, cone*, to *gon*, to *grone*, &c.; and *noon, soon, moon*, to *don*, &c. These classes of words are discussed below in § 54.

Cuckow and *prow* imperfect imitations of the French originals. not from the A.S. *gæc* nor the O.N. *gaukr*, but from the French *cucu*, now *coucou;* which leads me to observe that there is another old French word, *prowe* or *pru* = profit, which in Chaucer, in the form *prow*, rhymes repeatedly with *now* and *you*, which we now pronounce (Juu). Now the very form of *prowe* (given by Kelham), though I can find no evidence for a similar by-form of *cucu*, seems to imply *some* diphthongal sound which may—as I have suggested in a like case at the end of § 35 —have *struck the English ear* as resembling the English (ɔu) their nearest indigenous sound to represent it. (Compare *ponch* as the French representative of our familiar *punch*.) But here is the point: weighty evidence will be adduced by and by (§§ 51 to 56) tending to prove that *do, to, shoe*, were sounded by Chaucer with (uu), just as they are sounded at present; and Chaucer, whether it pleases our taste or not, did not make *cuckow* and *prow* rhyme with *do*, &c., but with *thow*, &c.

Of one of these words a derivative survives in our language, namely *prowess*, retaining, as I believe, the same diphthong as the root word had in Chaucer. The other, *cuckowe*, has changed; but is this difficult to account for? Not to mention our greatly increased intercourse with our French neighbours, and that at any rate their modern name for the bird is in accordance with the actual cry, we ourselves every spring take lessons in music from the songster himself, and have thus arrived at a more perfect onomatopœia than that which we first imported.

39 Negative arguments: first, *ou* words will not rhyme with (uu) words. Mr. Ellis however takes this written *ou* to be (uu). But besides the positive evidence above adduced to show that in a large class of words it stood for (ɔu), or some modification of that sound; the negative argument may also be fitly urged, and reasons be assigned for believing that *ou* was *not* (uu).

First then, we shall presently find another class of words which contained and contain (uu), and the sound is not expressed by *ou*, so that that sound is independently provided for; and moreover these words are never found rhyming with those that in A.S. are written with *ú*, and in E.E. with *ou* or *ow*: an argument of great weight, though it needs but few words to express it.

40 *Orthoepists do not make our ou = Italian u.* Then again, Smith, Hart, and other orthoepists are in the habit of referring to foreign languages to illustrate the nature of English sounds; but, except only the doubtful and limited assertion of Palsgrave above alluded to, no one of them makes the English *ou* or *ow* to be equivalent to the French *ou* or the Italian or German *u*.

41 *Cheke and Smith's account of ου.* Thirdly, both Cheke and Smith take the Greek ου (and Cheke, and possibly Smith,* the Latin *u* also) to be sounded as our *ou* in *foule* and *houle*, and expressly describe this as a compound sound. Smith says: "Ου diphthongus Græca, ou et ων. Ex o breui and u, diphthongum habebant Latini, quæ si non eadem, vicinissima certè est ου Græcæ diphthongo, et proxime accedit ad sonum *u* Latinæ," &c. See Ellis, p. 151 (where I think the "transliterations" are correct.) Smith's *o breuis* is exemplified elsewhere in the words *smock, horse, hop, sop, not, rob, bot, pop;* and I can see no sufficient ground for believing these words to have been at all otherwise sounded 300 years ago than they are now. His description therefore is at least approximately correct for (ɔu). Smith's expression, speaking of ου (de Ling. Græc. Pron., p. 38), "u facit Latinum quando producitur," I take to mean that when the (ɔu) sound is prolonged, the prolonged part of the compound is (uu), which it undoubtedly is.

42 *Smith's (uu) word is not written with ou.* But fourthly, when Smith elsewhere (de Ling. Angl. Script., p. 12) speaks of the Latin *u*—and in *this* passage I agree with Mr. Ellis (p. 167) that it is really (u) or (uu) that is intended—it is very remarkable that not one of the English words given as examples is spelt with *ou* or *ow*. Here they are: "Brevis but, sed;

---

* I mean that it is possible that Smith may have been inconsistent with himself, and entertained this notion when he wrote the passage quoted just below, which however he certainly did not entertain when he wrote that quoted in the next paragraph.

luk, fortuna ; buk, dama mas ; mud, limus ; ful, plenus ;
pul, deplumare ; tu, ad : *louga*, büt, ocrea ; lük, aspicere ;
bük, liber ; müd, ira aut affectus ; fůl, stultus ; půl, piscina ;
tü, duo, etiam." I need hardly explain that the words
which Smith thus writes are, in the usual spelling, *but, luck,
buck, mud, full, pull, to; boot, look, book, mood, fool, pool, two*
or *too*,—all, I believe with Mr. Ellis, sounded with (u) or
(uu) in Smith's time. It is strange indeed if, when a certain
sound was to be exemplified, and a multitude of words in
ou, as Mr. Ellis supposes, contained that sound, not one of
the fourteen examples was so spelt.

43 Fifth. Other grammarians distinguish (uu) and (əu words just as in modern English. Lastly, the grammarians on whose authority Mr. Ellis so much relies, and whom, as I believe, he so frequently misinterprets, furnish this additional argument against him, that they habitually observe a distinction in spelling between these (uu) and (əu) classes of words which Mr. Ellis confounds, and that distinction is just the same as in modern English. Thus Bullokar, 1580, writes *intoo, whoo, stool, tool, good, boot, broom, doo, dooth, look, crooked*, &c.; but *how, ground, douteth, found, towel, your, about, sound, bow* (vb.), *vowel, bowel, sower* (*i.e.* sour, German sauer). Bullokar's spelling is phonetic,[*] which greatly adds force to my argument; and other phoneticists—Gil and Butler who were later than Bullokar, and Smith and Hart who were earlier—all mark the same distinction. And so do other grammarians, who did not adopt a peculiar orthography; Palsgrave for example. And so did Chaucer: both his rhymes and, I may add, his spelling convict Mr. Ellis of error.

44 In a few words *ou* was = (uu). Were there then in Early English no words spelt with *ou* or *ow* and sounded otherwise than with (əu)? Certainly there were some sounded with (u) or (uu) or with (o) or (oo), chiefly words of French derivation and imperfectly Anglicised, many of which are still exceptionally pronounced. For example, *touch, country, double, trouble, course, discourse, flourish, courage:* so far

---

[*] Though I fail to discover any difference between the forms which he marks with the cedilla.

§ 45] ACCENTS IN ANGLO-SAXON. 31

back as the orthoepists will help us, we find these words already exceptional. Hart writes *dubl, kuntre, tuch,** *kura*ʒ, *diskurs*, with *u* = (u), I believe, and *y* = (uu); but he never writes *puud, muth, prouuns* (*i.e.* pronounce), *kunsel, konfuund, dut,* for *pound, mouth,* &c. Gil writes *trubl* and *flurish;* but *croun, doun, loud, proud, kloud*. And in many other words the evidence of early orthography combined with that of modern pronunciation—one portion of the evidence coming part way to meet the other—inclines me to think that from some cause, not always easy to ascertain or even conjecture, it became the fashion to spell certain words in a manner which in reality at *no* period represented the sound. On *would, should, could,* I will remark below, as also on *show, mow, blow, slow,* &c.: see §§ 57 and 47. But besides these, there are other words in which I doubt whether the *ou* was ever sounded (ɔu), as *youth, young, couple, souper* (Chaucer, also *soper* = supper), *source, bourne, mourn, mould,* &c.

45 *Disuse of Anglo-Saxon accents: the spoken words still distinguished.* As to the accents on *i* and *u* the facts appear to be these. There were in Anglo-Saxon classes of words different, though containing the same written vowel, and frequently, though not habitually, distinguished, namely by accents; † and these appear even in the earliest MSS. we possess, the *í* words being distinct from those with *i*, the *ú* words from those with *u*, and so on. In course of time these accents ceased to be written, which may not improbably have been because the scribes, accustomed to write Latin and French without any such diacritic signs, disliked the look of them, seeing clearly that accents at once stamped their fair calligraphy with an

---

* In one place he writes *touch*, either from force of habit, or else it is a mere misprint. Unfortunately such misprints are but too common in most early works of this class.

† Of course I do not mean that the accent was not very often omitted. It was in fact most commonly omitted in many or most MSS.; less no doubt through simple carelessness on the part of the writer, than because of the reader's supposed familiarity with the word. But still in certain words it very often appears; and it is a rare thing to find a word written with an accent which has no claim to one.

appearance of vulgarity by showing so conspicuously that the writing was only in the language of the *profanum vulgus*. But whatever the cause was, the fact remains that accents disappeared: very few are to be found in the Ormulum, none in Laȝamons Brut, the Ancren Riwle, and all later writers. But before long some of the same classes of words are again found distinguished in writing, and even more regularly than before, though with a different distinction. No substitute was provided for the accented *í;* but we find the words which in Anglo-Saxon had *ú* afterwards written with *ou* or *ow*, apparently for no other reason than to distinguish them from the *u* words; this new orthography coming into use probably about the close of the 13th century. Who first introduced it, or in what part of England it arose, I have not had time to investigate, if indeed these questions can now be answered; but whenever it appeared, it was only a new mode of representing a difference of sound which itself was as old as the language.

46 We proceed now to consider two other classes of words. And let us approach them on the side of the symbols, thus.

<small>The A.S. *á* became *o*.</small> I turn to the A.S. dictionaries, Bosworth's and Grein's, and going right through them I find the following list of words spelt with á—a complete list, I believe, of all the words with á (excluding derivatives) that survived to or beyond Chaucer's time, except *acsian*, which Grein is in error in accenting, and with five other apparent exceptions which I will mention: á, ác, án, ár, ágan, ágen, bán, bát, bláwan, brád, cláð, fá, fám, flá, gá, gár, gást, gát, gráf, gránian, grápian, hál, hálig, hám, hár, hás, hát, hláf, hálford, hwá, lá, lám, lár, láð, má, mára, máwan, ná, nán, rád, ráp, sár, sáwan, sáwel, sceáwian, snáw, stán, swá, swápan, tá, tácn, twá, þá, wá, wár, wráð; also certain vernal preterits as arás, bát, glád, sceán, wrát. The later forms of these words are—*o* (ever), oak, ōne (pronounced as we still sound it in the compounds alone, atone, and only; though it has passed through the form of oōn into wŭn), oar, own (verb and adj.), bone, boat, blow (Lat. flare), broad (which we now call *brawd*), cloth (now

clōth), foe, foam, flo (= arrow), go, goar, ghost, goat, grove, groan, grope, whole, holy, home, hoar, hoce (as it is still called in Devonshire, though polite English has corrupted in into *hoarse*), hōt (which since Chaucer's time we have shortened into hŏt), loaf, lōrd (now *lŏrd*), whō—now (Huu), but in Chaucer's time (whō) rhyming with *mo*,—lo, loam, lore, loth, mo, more, mow (vb.), no, nōne (now pronounced *nŭn*), road, rope, sore, sow, soul, show, snow, swope—now swoop—stone, so, toe, token, twō—now (tuu)*—tho, woe, ore-weed (a term still used in Devonshire for sea-weed), wrōth (now more commonly wrŏth); and the preterits arose, bote (from bite), glode (from glide), shōne (now shŏn), and wrote.

47 *Apparent exceptions really Old Norse words, not Anglo-Saxon.* The five words excluded from the list are those which the Old Norse has modified or superseded, just as the above words in the Scottish dialect,—ane, ain, aik, hame, rape, bane, stane, &c.—are not really modern forms of the Anglo-Saxon words above quoted, but of the Old Norse einn, eigin, eyk, heimi, reip, bein, steinn, &c., with ei (eei). Our five words are spátl, which the Old Norse spýta—now pronounced (spiita) but of old probably (spyyta)—has transformed into *spittle*; and swān, swāt, wāc, wāfian, which the Old Norse sveinn, sveiti, veikr, and veifa have ousted altogether, becoming swain, sweat (sweet) now (swet), weak (week) now (wiik), and waive and waver.†

48 *Mr. Murray's view of the Scandinavian element in the Northern dialects.* Mr. J. A. H. Murray says, "There seems ground to regard many of the characteristics of the northern dialect which currently pass as Danish as having been original elements of the North Angle speech, due to the fact that this dialect was, like the Frisian, one which formed a connecting link between the Scandinavian and Germanic branches. Such

---

* It is doubtless the influence of the *s* preceding that has changed the sound of (o) into ou in *so*, *fass*, *sove*, &c., while *sovd* changed into *swon* finds its exact analogue in *twā* (twoo), as the Devonian form of *o*, &c.

† Stapan had the by-forms slōpan and slepan, the last of which above has survived.

characteristics would of course be strengthened and increased by the influx of Danish and Norwegian settlers, but the influence of these was necessarily at first confined to particular localities, and only gradually and at a later period affected the northern dialect as a whole."* These views are probably correct; but there can scarcely be a doubt that in England south of the Humber the forms *spittle*, &c. were due to the influence of the Danish invaders rather than to that of the Northern Angles, unless indeed we extend Mr. Murray's hypothesis to the whole of the Angles, instead of limiting it to the northern division.

49 Inasmuch then as, with only these five exceptions so easily accounted for, *all* the Anglo-Saxon words in *á* which survived to or beyond the age of Chaucer are now pronounced, according to the tradition of *all our Southern dialects* (for I resolutely hold to this argument), with (o); and there is no reason to suspect that there has been any change since Chaucer's time; and in Chaucer too these

<small>The (o) sound confirmed by French and Italian.</small> words rhyme with French words like *chose*, or words from the French like *rose* and *suppose*; nor is there any reason to suspect that the French *chose*, *rose*, &c.—especially as confirmed by the Italian *cosa*, *rosa*, &c.—have failed to preserve at least approximately the true ancient sound of their principal vowel; we seem to have pretty good ground for concluding that these words in the 14th century were sounded with (o); and there is no sufficient evidence that they were not sounded exactly the same in the earliest English.

50 <small>Chaucer's gat-toothed.</small> (Consideration of the pronunciation of the Anglo-Saxon *á* will help us to decide the meaning of Chaucer's much disputed epithet of the Wif of Bathe—*gattoothed*; at least it enables us decisively to set aside the explanation of the word as signifying *goat-toothed*, whatever that may mean. Gát (goot) would never be shortened into *gat* (gat), but into *got* (got), whereas all the MSS. appear to have *gat* or *gate*. The true sense is *gate-toothed*, where however we must bear in mind that

* *Dialect of the Southern Counties of Scotland*, Historical Introduction. p. 24.

gate, from *go*, originally means, not a wooden barrier, but a passage: see my edition of the Castle of Love, Gloss. s.v. ʒat. The compound signifies therefore that the "worthi womman" had teeth, not set in close rank, but with gateways, interstices, between them. I am glad to see that Dr. Morris similarly explains the word.)

51 *Anglo-Saxon words in ó sounded with (uu), modern English oo.* Let us go again to our dictionaries. Now we find another set of words with *ó*, of which the following is, I believe, a complete list of such as reached Chaucer; blód, blówan, bóc, bóg, bósm, bót, bróc, bróðor, cóc, cófa (?), cól, dóhtor, dóm, dón, cóʒoð, cóh,ców, flód, flór, flówan, fóðor, fóstur, fót glóf, glóm, gód, gós, grówan, hóc, hóf, hóp, hróf, hróst, hwópan, lócian, mód, móður, mónað, mór, nón, nósu (?), óðer, pól, ród, Róm, róse, sceótan, scólu, sóð, sófte (?), sóna, stól, stów, tó, tóð, wód, wóh, wrótan; and the preterites forsóc, sceóc, stód. Of twenty-six of these the 19th century representatives are—boot ("it boots not"), cool, doom, do, youth, yew, you, gloom, goose, hoof, hoop, roof, roost, whoop, mood, moon, noon, pool, rood, school ("a school of mackerel"), sooth, soon, stool, to, tooth, and root ("to root up"), all with (uu); twelve others we pronounce with *oŏ* (u)—book, bosom, brook, cook, foot, good, hook, look, shoot, forsook, shook, stood; seven others have the *ŭ* (ɔ) of *but*—blood, brother, flood, glove, mother, month, other; and of these nineteen ten are found in the Ormulum, *all* with the long vowel. Of the remainder two (wód and wóg) are now obsolete; of two (bóg and dóhtor) the guttural following, which has now disappeared, has disturbed the vowel, so that from the sound of *bough* or *daughter* we can conclude nothing. The few that remain blow ("full blown"), flow, grow, slow; fother, foster child; floor, moor; cove, nose, Rome, rose, soft. I have not time to discuss, beyond observing that we know *Rome*, which was *Rome* also in the Chanson de Roland, to have continued as (Ruum) down to Shakespeare's time. The forty-five words already discussed, to which, judging from analogy, hól, hróc, and sceó should be added, are sufficient for my purpose, which is to fix the sound of (uu) for them all.

52 *This (uu) confirmed by Dutch and German.* And if my readers are not tired of Dutch and German, I will call their attention to the following list:—

Engl.	Du.	Germ.
blood	bloed	Blut
blow	bloeijen	blühen
book	boek	Buch
bosom	boezem	Busen
brother	broeder	Bruder
cool	koel	kühl
doom	doem (Kil.)	-thum
do	doen	thun
flood	vloed	Fluth
floor	vloer	Flur
flow	vloeijen	—
fother	voeder	Fuder
foster (child)	voedster (kind)	—
foot	voet	Fuss
good	goed	gut
grow	groeijen	—
hood	hoed	Hut
hook	hoek (Kil.)	Huck
hoof	hoef	Huf
hoop	hoepel	—
rook	roek	Rucke
mood	moed	Muth
mother	moeder	Mutter
pool	poel	Pfuhl
rood	roede	Ruthe
shoe	schoen	Schuh
stool	stoel	Stuhl
to	toe	zu
wode (adj.)	woede (s.)	Wuth
root up	wroeten	—

Thus, as in the case of our *i* words, the Dutch and German languages lend an emphatic confirmation to the evidence of our own almost universal tradition as to the sound of these words with (uu).

53 *Did* not a reduplicate preterit. (The settlement of the ancient pronunciation of *do* as (duu), as at present, enables us to get rid of the erroneous notion that *did* is a reduplicate preterit. If, as I believe with Mr. Ellis, the A.S. *y* was sounded (y), *dyde*, the old preterit of *dón*, was simply a weak preterit, regularly formed except as to modification of the vowel by the "umlaut," precisely as in *jung, jünger*, &c. It is not really the same but a different question whether in weak verbs generally the termination *-de* is derived from the verb *do*. This notion is based on the fact that there are two *d*s in the dual and plural of the Mœso-Gothic preterit; the terminations of that tense being—

-da	-dedu	-dedum
-des	-deduts	-deduth
-da		-dedun

But in the M.G. for *to do* the preterit in full runs thus—

Sing.	Du.	Plu.
tawida	tawidedu	tawidedum
tawides	tawideduts	tawideduth
tawida		tawidedun

And here we lose the apparent reduplication, or approach to reduplication, which we have in the English *dyde* or *dide*, the root *tau* and the termination *dedu* being by no means so similar. Moreover, if that is the derivation, why should *rodida* mean "I *did* speak" rather than "I *do* speak"? And the word *di-de* itself when so explained becomes do - di-de do ÷ do - di-de do - do - do - di-de, and so on: a manifest absurdity. It seems far more satisfactory to consider the dental *d* (or *t*) of the preterit akin to the dental *d* (or *t* or the cognate dental-nasal-liquid *n*) of the past participle. It is true that the French express "I will speak" by "I have to speak," *parler-ai*, and "we have to speak" by *parler-(av)ons*, and have in course of time run together these and similar pairs of words into single words; but we are not warranted in pushing this analogy so far as to contend that every inflexion in every language was originally a separate and distinct word. I should much rather believe that, letters having a force of their own (as the sibilant in εἰς and πρός for example suitably expresses the idea of motion combined with that of the radical ἐν or πρό), the explosive *t* or *d* or the kindred nasal indicated interjection-wise a sense of relief when the action was finished and the work accomplished; and this equally in ἀγαπητός and *amatus*, *geliebt* and *loved* (pt.), *liebte*, *lufode*, *dyde*, *done* and τυπτόμενος. It would be digressing too far to trace a like adaptation of sound to sense in *amant-*, *amand-*, τυπτοντ- (tiip'toond), τυπεντ- (tii'pend), liebend, lufiand, &c.)

54 A.S. *á* and *ó* both *o* in Chaucer, yet distinct in sound. We have already seen one class of words in which the A.S. *á* stands for (oo) or (ọọ), and now we find the A.S. *ó* in another considerable class represents the sound of (uu); and, as I believe, these words were always so pronounced. Mr. Ellis, however, imagines that *do*, *to*, *schoo*, *doom*, *soone*, &c., were pronounced with (oo), like *go*, *so*, *mo*, *stoon*, *noon* (adj.), &c. These two classes of words are, in fact, totally distinct; but misled by the mere *written* language, and too implicitly believing that "the orthography shows the sound" (p. 255, heading), Mr. Ellis has confounded them, regardless of the distinction in their pronunciation now and certainly for some centuries, and of the distinction in their orthography in A.S., and utterly deaf to the clamorous protests of their continental kinsmen. In Chaucer it is true these classes of words are spelt alike, but pronounced alike they are not. Innumerable in Chaucer are the rhymes of *go*, *i-go*, *so*, *also*, *woo* (= woe), *tho*, *mo*, *foo*, *fro*, *too* (= toe), *slo* (= sloe), *who*, *two* (= two), *ho*, *no*, *flo* (= arrow); and very numerous those of *do*, *i-do*, *fordo*, *to*, *thereto*, *and schoo*. Once only in all the Canterbury Tales does *do* rhyme with *so*, once only *i-do* with *ho*, once *therto* with *mo*; but the numeral *two* seems somewhat shifting towards its present pronunciation, for twice it rhymes with *do* and twice with *i-do*. Again we have *brode, loode* (s), *glod, bistrood,* rhyming together, and *rood* (vb.), *abode, prentyshood,* are of the same class: but not once in all the Cant. Ta. do these rhymes with *food, stood, understode, mood, wode, hode, blode, flood.* Again, *cloke, poke* (s.), *broke, smoke* rhyme, as do *strook* and *oak;* but none of these rhyme with *schook, cooke, took, wook, awook, quook, forsook, look, pook.* Again, *oon, aloon, anoon, echoon, ilkeone, everychon, bone, gone, agoon, crone, schon* (vb.), *ton* (= toes), *lone* (= loan), *moone* (= moan), *persone, stone,* and some proper names, furnish an immense number of rhymes; *doon, i-doon, soone, boone, moone* (= luna), *spoon, noon* (= midday), also a large number: only four imperfect rhymes are there, and for these *doon* is responsible. *Goos* rhymes with *schoos* and with *loos* (adj.); but not once with *loos* (= laus), *cloos* (adj.), *close* (vb.), *toos* (= toes), *glose,* "*chose,*" *rose, hose, nose, pose, suppose, purpose, dispose. Swoote,* Chaucer's epithet of April showers, and the pronunciation of which is tolerably fixed by the Dutch *zoet* and German *süss,* rhymes with *roote, bote* (= remedy), and *foot;* none of these rhyme even once with *noote, rote, coote* (= coat), *bot* (vb.), *throte, hote, woot, not* (vb.), *boot* (= boat), *wroot, goot, otc-s, smoot.* Lastly, with *sooth* we have *tooth* rhyming, and *doth* (now dŭth : but not *goth* (= goeth), *cloth, loth, wroth, bothe, oth :* once only *forsothe* rhymes with *bothe.* So perfectly distinct were the (*oo*) and the (*uu*) words in Chaucer's language, however spelt.

An examination of the first five thousand lines of Roberde of Brunne's Handlyng Synne, for the *o* words, gives just such results as are derived from Chaucer. *Mo, go, oo* (= aye, *too, slo* = slay, *þo* (adv.), *þo* (pron.), *fro,* rhyme with one another exclusively: *do* rhymes regularly with *to* and its compounds: *two* rhymes once with *slo,* once with *do :* but *so* and *also,* curiously enough, and quite contrary to Chaucer's usage, rhyme only with *do* and *to,* except once only with the doubtful numeral *two.** In like manner *noon, soon, shoon* rhyme with *don* (inf.) and *done* (part.), never with *bone, stone, gone, one* with its compounds, &c. Once only the part. *done* rhymes with *none*, and twice with nouns of French derivation in -*un* (which R. of Br. writes more commonly than -*on* or -*oun*). So *fote* (= foot), *boot* (= remedy), rhyme with each other, but never with *hote* (adj.), *hote* (= promise), *smote, grote, wrote, wote, note, þrote*, and so on, though a bad rhyme, such as *come* with *gone, goste* with *hast*, occurs here and there.

55 *Occasional exceptions mistaken by Mr. Ellis for the rule.* As to one imperfect rhyme here and there, any reader of modern English verse might well be surprised if there were not in Chaucer any such maculæ—

quas aut incuria fudit,
Aut humana parum cavit natura.*

With such imperfect rhymes Chaucer seems to have been content in dealing with proper names and foreign words. Thus while *Amazōne* and *Salamōn* alone occur, rhyming with *stone*, &c.; we have not only *Palamōn* rhyming with *anoon*, &c., but also *Palamoun* rhyming with *doun* and *toun* (eleven of the former rhymes, eighteen of the latter). *Plato* rhymes once with *tho*, once with *to;* *Juno* with *fordo; principio* with *schoo; Cupido, Placebo,*

change the (o) into (u) in all of them. They all hesitated, *two* finally gave way, but *so* and *also* stood firm in the original sound after ejecting the semi-vowel.

* A lady has kindly collected for me a few such faulty rhymes from some of our 19th century poets:—

KEATS: *wood, flood; loll, poll; Arabian, man; trees, essences; these, offices; exhalations, cons; beautiful, cull; strawberries, butterflies.*

SHELLEY: *hail, majestical; death, path; shun, on; now, glow; feet, yet; abode, brotherhood; burning, morning.*

COLERIDGE: *guest, dismist; hear, Mariner; groan, one; fear, were; full, dull; fair, are; humming, women.*

WORDSWORTH: *flood, wood; gone, alone; dead, laid; ere, near; low, fro; long, hung; forth, earth; now, low; read, abroad; come, home; groves, loves; breath, underneath; year, fair.*

TENNYSON: *early, barley; weary, airy; brow, snow; close (vb.), house; ran, swan; was, pass; wood, bud.*

W. MORRIS: *afar, war; were, near; heard, afeard; bear, rear; stood, blood; gone, alone; throne, upon; below, bow (vb.); here, artificer.*

and *Themalco* with the somewhat doubtful *two*; *Ekko* and *Erro* (= Hero) with *woo* (= woe). Yet, strange to say, it is upon these foreign words, yielding such inconsistent evidence, that Mr. Ellis chiefly relies. His view is mainly, if not even exclusively, based on the single rhyme of *schoo* with *principio* (p. 266)!

56 Recapitulation on 'O' words. The facts then as to these '*o*' words may be briefly re-stated thus: There are words with similar *written* terminations which clearly pair off into two classes, which in Chaucer refuse to rhyme with each other; of these classes the vowels are fixed by universal English tradition as (o) or some modification of that sound for the first, and (u) for the second; this tradition being confirmed by French and Italian tradition for the first, and by German and Dutch tradition for the second. The hypothesis that they were sounded with (o) and (u) respectively satisfies all the conditions of the problem, save only the very few exceptions above noted. It has been suggested that these two *o*s are simply the Italian *ò* and *ó*. But there is this grave objection, that those two can rhyme; in Dante they rhyme habitually; while, as we have seen, in Chaucer and other English poets the two classes are kept distinct.

57 *Could, would, should.* This seems to be the proper place to remark on the forms *could*, *would*, and *should*. There can be little doubt that the similarity of grammatical use of these three words has affected the spelling of all three, and exceptionally the pronunciation of one of them. The pronunciation of *would* and *should*, except that in quite modern times we drop the *l*,* has been the same for at least three centuries, the vowel being u or uu. Thus Gil, 1621, writes *shuld*, with u uu; and Hart, 1569, writes *uld* and *shuld* with u Gil's u or through carelessness or misprint? *uld* and *shuld*; and Chaucer's forms and those of other E. E. writers are *wolde, wold, woolde, sholde, scholde, schold, shulde, ssolde:* only these, I believe; at any rate, none with *ou*. And the A.S. forms were *wolde* and

---

* Cooper, 1685, condemns *wuds* and *we't*, for *would-t*, as belonging to the "barbara dialectus."

sceolde, never with *ú*. So far therefore as the testimony of ancient orthography and of these orthoepists goes, the vowel was not (ɔu). *Could* on the other hand is in A. S. *cúde*, and in Chaucer and his contemporaries *coude, coupe, cowde* (or with *k* or *th*); and it has these forms only, the vowel being the same as in *dún*, down, *hús*, house, &c. Nowa-days we sound all three words alike. We may therefore not unreasonably infer that the *o* in the A.S. *wólde* and *sceólde* had the accent (though I do not find it so written in the dictionaries*), and that these words have always in the "Englisce spræc" had the sound of (uu) or later (u), and yet, as to their written form, they borrowed a *u* from *coude*, which nevertheless failed to affect their sound: that *coude* on the other hand, in sound, but not in writing, exchanged its diphthongal (ɔu) for the (uu) or (u) of its comrade auxiliaries; as it also, in too slavish imitation, assumed the *l*, which was radical to them, but to which it had no claim. It may be added that this *l* in *could* is sometimes sounded in the West of England; and, curiously enough, Hart also sounded it. At least we find the word, even in his phonetic writing, as *kuld*, or *kuld*, or once (by mistake, no doubt) *kould*.

58. Now, as I have above assigned at least plausible reasons for believing that the *i* of A.S. and Chaucer's long *i* (I am speaking of the written symbols now, were sounded (ɔi , and not (ii), I shall not be expected to accept Mr. Ellis's view as to *ai* and *ei*, that these were both sounded ʼai . For if so, we could not but have had *i* and *ei* or *ai* at least occasionally rhyming. There is not an instance of the kind in Chaucer, nor have I noticed one in any other poetry, always excepting the two words *die* and *dry*, which had also the other but rarer forms *dey* and *dreye*. The latter of these I cannot account for: the former is simply

---

* Grein is the best authority as to accents, yet not always correct. If he is right in refusing the accent to *wolde* and *scolde*, as analogous forms to the Ger. *wollte* and *sollte*, then these are the only A.S. words I have met with, which have an unaccented *o* that becomes (uu) in the later stages of the language.

the O.N. *deyja, ek dey*. What sound then is represented

<small>The symbols *ai* and *ei* sounded as in modern French.</small> —or what sounds—by *ai* and *ei* (or *ay* and *ey*)? These symbols are at present pronounced alike in French; and that they were pronounced alike in early English (as Mr. Ellis admits) the rhymes of Chaucer and the frequent interchange of these digraphs in writing one and the same word, seem conclusively to prove. And if again we appeal to tradition, the traditional sound in both countries is, with certain exceptions, (ee) or (ee), as in *vain, vein ; faites, veine*. But let us as before examine a few of the words themselves; for, as I have remarked of previous classes of words, when a few are fixed, the rhymes of Chaucer and other E. E. poets will show that these few draw a multitude of others with them.

59 Now the verb *dey* (= die), as has just been pointed out, is the O.N. *deyja* (deei'ja). *May* (= maid) is the O.N. *mey*. *Obey* is from *obedire* through *obéir*. *Journey, valley, chimney*,

<small>Pr = f from the O.N. and O.Fr. originals of certain of these words.</small> are the Fr. *journée, vallée, cheminée*, which have had that termination (as written) unchanged for at least the last six centuries. The words *lay* (= law) and *fey* (= faith) are in O.Fr. *leis* and *fei* (feis ?) or *feid* or *fé*, the former of which—to glance at the derivation, a point which Mr. Ellis far too commonly overlooks—is evidently the Latin *legi-s* with the guttural dropped, and the latter a syncopated form of *fidei ;* and these in the Chanson de Roland are in assonance with *reis* (= king, from *regi-s*), *fedeil* (from *fidelis*), *mei* (Lat. mei), *meis* (Lat. mensis), *creit* (Lat. credit), &c. *Array* (vb.) was in O.Fr. *areer*. *Moneye* was *moneie* Burguy), or *monnoie*, and *oi* we know was pronounced (oee or (wee), with no 'a' in it, *Nobleye* is *noblee* in Kelham. From the noun *preye* is the verb *preer* in the Conquest of Ireland. And these twelve words draw with them *way, away, alway, they, say, day, lay*, (vb.), *bewrey, may, May, jay, play, abbaye, faeye*, and many besides; all of which indiscriminately and constantly rhyme with one another. In the Ormulum, which, according to Dr. Morris, exhibits the Lincolnshire dialect of the early part of the thirteenth century, we find a distinction be-

tween daȝȝ and maȝȝ, and þeȝȝ and weȝȝe, of which there is no trace in Chaucer. (See § 65.)

60 *The endings (eid), (eth), and (en), thus ascertained; with further independent evidence in many cases.* If then these -*ay* words are fixed, the preterites of the verbs among them, *deyed, pleide, affrayed, preyde,* &c., will fix other words rhyming with these, such as *maid* (O.Du. meeghd) and *brayde*. And in like manner we are taught how to sound *fayth* by *deyth, seyth, layth*.

Next, words in (*ein*). The infinitive of *sey* (*see*) is of course *seyn* (*seen*). *Sweyn*, as I have above observed, is the O.N. *sveinn*, which is nearly (*sweeidn*). *Tweyn* and *reyne* (= rain) are certainly contracted from *tweegen* and *regen*, the tweȝȝenn and reȝȝn of the Orm., in neither of which is there any vestige of an (a) sound; nor is there any original (a) in *atteyne*, from attingo, *distreyne*, from distringo, *desdeyne*, from disdignor (= dedignor), *peyne* from pœna, *Maudeleyne*, from Magdalene, *feyne*, from fingo, *veyne*, from vena. And these enable us to fix *vein* (adj.), *certeyn, Spayne, soverayn, agayn, brayn, greyne, cheyne, compleyne*, &c.; for all these indiscriminately and constantly rhyme with the above and with one another. And as to *certaine* and *vilaine*, these are found in the old French song by Le Vidame de Chartres rhyming with *maine - mène*, from mener, Du. mennen, where there is clearly no (a).

61 *Evidence from Meigret, and the assonances of O.Fr. poetry.* Now in Old French we find, as Mr. Payne has pointed out, words occasionally spelt with *e* which more commonly have *ai*, as *lesser, reson, treter, cler, set* (= sait), &c.* And if we turn to Meigret we find that many of the words usually spelt with *ai* are by him phonetically spelt with *e*: grammére, jamés, més, &c., and in particular fés, fét, fére, fézons, &c. Moreover in the Chanson de Roland this verb *faire* and its compounds are commonly assonant with *e* words—*perte, perdet, mueles, apelet, tere, bele,* &c. In like manner *repaire* and *esclairet* are assonant with *deserte, herberges,* and other *e*

---

* See also the numerous rhymes of *ai* with *e* words in French poetry, which Mr. Payne has collected: Transactions of the Philological Society for 1868-9, p. 387 sq.

words; and *heir* (= Eng. heir) with *reis, mei,* &c. And these words in Old French songs rhyme with *de bon aire* and *paire* (= pair). And with *debonaire, paire, repeyre, heir, faire* (s.) we have rhyming in Chaucer *faire* (adj.), *cir, dispeir,* &c.

But as Meigret fixes for his age the sound of *jamais*, and already in the Chanson de Roland *jamais* is in assonance with *desert, Samuel, apres,* and other *e* words; *jamais*, together with *fais* and *fait* (see Wright's Political Poems, i. 302) fixes *Caleys*, which in turn is found rhyming with *paleys* and *deys*, and these again with *burgeys, harneys*, &c. And in the Ch. de Rol. *deiz* and *palefreiz* are associated with *soleilz, aveir, franceis* (It. francese), *dreit,* &c., and never with any (a) words.

62 _{Three exceptions in French; Palsgrave on *ai*.} Do I mean then to deny that the written *ai* was ever (ai)? Certainly not. There are for instance those three words mentioned by Meigret, which modern fashion, consistently with their derivation too, would or does write with *puncta diæresis*—*aÿmant*, adamant or loadstone (now aimant), *aÿdant** (now aidant), and *haïr*; to which *païen, païs* (now pays pai-is), *traïr, traïson, traïtre* (now traitre) may be added, the sound of the last of which is clear when we find it in assonance with *olive, ocire*, &c.; and the forms *païs, traïr*, &c., are capable of like proof, which rhyme elsewhere supports. Then again *faire* itself, though no doubt commonly *fere*, occurs once in the Ch. de Rol. (in accordance with its etymology also *facere*) in assonance with (a) words—*Carles, marche, message;* and so *repaire* once with *visage, esguardent*, &c.; though in the Conquest of Ireland this verb has always *ei*. And we know by instances just mentioned *aimant, aidant, traitre*, that the (ai) can pass into *ee*; of which too the O.Fr. *gueter* (now guetter) and the phrase *aux aguets* from O.N. *gæta* (gaaita, to watch, is a proof, and *ay*- ever, from O.N. *æ aai*. And when Palsgrave says that "*Ai* in the frenche tong is sounded . . . *a* distinctly and the *i* shortly and confusely," one can have no difficulty in seeing that

---

* 'A Paris dans le peuple on dit souvent *ade*.' Littré, s.v.

while there are many more exceptions than those he specifies,* his rule applies without doubt to all words in which the *ai* is followed by *ll* (as even in modern French, e.g., *travailler*), or *ge* (in which modern French keeps the simple *a*). The word *sage* or *saige*, for instance—and Palsgrave directs a faint *i* to be inserted after the *a* in words in -*age*, even if it is not written—occurs in the Ch. de Rol. in the form *saive* (i.e. sapiens) in assonance with (a) words, *marche, Carles*, &c.; as also *bataille, vaille, asaillet*, occur only in assonance with (a) words.

63 *No exceptions in Chaucer, where ai words rhyme with one another without distinction.* But is this ever the case in Chaucer? For some time I imagined it might be so, that Chaucer's *travayle* and *batayle* would be sounded like the French words, but *veyl, sayle, ayle* (vb.) as at present; but having run through the Cant. Ta. once more expressly to examine the rhymes with this termination, I am forced to a different conclusion; for I find the words with a radical (a) are twenty-four in number—*vitaille* (= victualia), *hayl* (= hagel), *aveyle* (from valere), &c.; those with a radical (e) or (i) are six—*veyle* (from velum), *sayle* (from segel), *merveile* (from mirabile), and *chamayle* (Ch. de Rol., cameil, from camelus), &c. But these six words rhyme with one another even less frequently than with the others: six times with one another, ten times with the former class. It is therefore impossible that there can be a distinction in the pronunciation of these classes.

64 Was -*ail* then sounded with (ee) or with (ai)? With (ee), I reply. First, the analogy of Chaucer's spelling of the words in -*ai*, -*aid*, -*aith*, -*air*, -*ais*, points to (ee). Secondly, in six of these words the etymology will fully account for the sound of (e), not for that of (a). Thirdly, of two of the same words (*cunseill* and *merveill*) the as-

---

* He specifies futures in -*ray*, as sounded like -*rey*, but also in the Introduction, p. xviii., he says: "in stede of *ai*, they sounde most communly *ee*." And so Meigret gives us *er, eyr, eymer, eyt, veyr*, &c. And we must not forget that a multitude of words now written with *ai* had *ei* (oee) in Palsgrave's time —*anglois, francois, monnoie, povement*, &c., and especially all imperfect and conditional tenses.

§ 66]   'AI' AND 'EI' WORDS.   47

sonances of the Ch. de Rol. are solely with (e) words.
Fourthly, these same assonances show that one of the others (like *faire* mentioned just above) was wavering in its sound even in French: *ventaille* (Chaucer's *adventayle*) is associated with *hastet*, *vasselage*, &c., and elsewhere with *sele*, *perdre*, &c. Fifthly, I find *apareillez*, so spelt in the same poem. Lastly, if the Lancelot of the Laik may be quoted as an authority, I find there the forms *batell* and *travell*—clearly an (e) and not an (ai) sound—and *bataill* rhyming with the adjective *haill*, which is the O. N. *heill* (Iceidl).

Etymology, as sonances, &c., all show the sound to have been (ee).

65 Time forbids me to examine the rest of the *ai* terminations, *-aim*, *-eint*, *-cisc*, *-ait*, *-eive*, all of which, either from analogy alone, or for that and other reasons, I believe to have been pronounced with (*ee*); but one inquiry must not be omitted. What of Palsgrave's assertion that *rayne*, *payne*, *fayne*, *disdayne*, were pronounced like the French *ai* as opposed to *ei*, namely, the "*a* distinctly and the *i* shortly and confusely"? Why, I take his words to exhibit a simply local or temporary fashion, which did not take a firm hold even on himself; for he in his vocabulary writes *peyne*, as he also gives both *cheyne* and *chayne*. But from whatever cause, and to whatever extent Palsgrave distinguished *ai* from *ei* in English, such distinction was utterly unknown to Chaucer.

Palsgrave again on ai.

66 Obviously, that *ai* in Chaucer's time *was* the representative of (ai), and that at an earlier period it *had been* so, are widely different propositions. The former I deny; the latter, in many cases, I admit.

Many of these ai words may have had an older sound (ai).

Though the proofs are numberless that from the 14th century, or earlier to the present day, *chain* has been sounded like *pain*, and the latter, from *pana*, has no radical *a*, nor is likely to have been ever sounded with *a*; *chain* on the contrary, from *catena*, had a radical *a*, and one cannot doubt that *kaena*, *tshaena*, *tshaina*, were early stages through which the word passed. So *facere*, that is *fakere*, passed through *faere*, *faire*, to the modern *faire* *feer*,

In like manner, though no (a) remains in the modern *day*, it exists in the Germ. *Tag*, Du. *dag*, O. N. *dagr*, M. G. *dags*, &c., as well as in the A. S. *dag* and *dah*, from which *dæg* and *da*ȝȝ (Orm.) lead on to *day* (dee). Many other words now sounded with (ee) or (ee) are shown by their etymology to have undergone like change of sound,—*air*, Lat. aer, *chair*, Lat. cathedra, *Spain*, Lat. Hispania, *champaign* from campanus, &c.

67 *Summary of arguments on ai words.* In taking leave of these *ai* words it is important to observe that, varied as are the sources of information to which I appeal, there is little clashing as to the general results they yield, which lends to the several results most weighty confirmation, based as they are on entirely independent evidence. Rhymes in Early English, Early Scotch, Early French; orthography, especially of the Ormulum; distinct statements of old grammarians; assonances in Early French poetry; etymologies; modern pronunciation of German, Dutch, Icelandic, French; and above all, the pronunciation of most of the English dialects*—all these for the most part harmonize in the conclusions which they dictate. Early rhymes habitually associate these words—*may, dey, lay, fay, obey* (above § 29). Icelandic pronunciation fixes the first two; assonances and etymology fix the other three; modern French pronunciation also bears witness to the last; and these sources of information all give us the *same* sound, while modern English pronunciation fully accords both as to these and others that rhyme with them. We shall find *entirely independent*, though less various evidence as to the vowel sound in *knee, see, he, me*, &c.; and these words—

---

* I must notice at least in a foot-note the objection that in Middlesex and some adjoining counties words written with *ai* are often sounded with (ai) (ei) or (eei). But in fact this sound being given to words with the simple *a* as well as to words with *ai*—to *pane, lane, mane*, as much as to *pain, lain, main*—the argument proves too much, and therefore nothing. If *ail*, A.S. *egl*, Ger. *Segl*, O.N. *segl*, &c., with no radical (ai), is now locally sounded with (aeel), the simplest solution is that this (regen) has become (reen), then (reen), then (reein), and that this the prevailing pronunciation has then been corrupted into (reein).

though Mr. Ellis would sound them (kne), (se), (He), (me), &c.—never rhyme with the class we have just been discussing.

68 '**A**' **words:** Chaucer's *a* certainly not *ee*, but some (*a*) sound.
Now it needs but a slight acquaintance with Chaucer to discover that many pairs of words which rhyme now—one word containing one of the last discussed diphthongs and the other the simple *a*—never rhyme in Chaucer. Thus *travayl, aveille, apparaille*, never rhyme with *dale, vale, tale;* nor *eyr, despeir, faire* (s. or adj.), *debonaire*, with *fare, care, snare, tare;* and so on. Moreover many of these words with the single vowel are of French derivation, and there is no reason to suspect that tradition has not preserved in them in French the true pronunciation of (a); and hence it is likely that such words, though now sounded with (ee) or (ee), yet, having certainly undergone some change, were sounded in the 14th century with some (a) sound; so that also the Dutch *faam, naam, dal, taal, aap, staat, waar* (s.), *waken, maken*, at least approximately represent the English pronunciation of these words for several centuries.

But a change having taken place in the sound of so large a class of words, is there any means of ascertaining when that change took place?

69 The change from (a) to the present (ee) earlier in Scotland than in England, probably through O N influence.
It was certainly effected much sooner in Scotland than in England, and mainly, I believe, arising from the fact (see above, § 48) that the North Angle dialect was so close akin to the Old Norse. In the Lancelot of the Laik, in Ratis Raving, and other early Scottish poems, we find words rhyming habitually which never rhymed in Chaucer, nor even in Ben Jonson, though some of them did frequently in Spenser. Thus *grace, place, pace*, or *paiss, space, ss, face*, all (a) words in Chaucer, rhyme with *fadyrless, makless, perches* (purchase*), wantonase, gudlynes, lavelynes, meknes, ryches*, &c.* *Maade* (b.), *degrade, raide*

* Mr. Murray suggests, with some plausibility, that the (a) and (ee) classes of words met on the c(?)atern ground(?) of(?) the Nor(?)th, of (?) power, &c. being sounded much like the English, ... , ... (a) (e, bb), and so on. This, however, seems to apply only to the e vowels.

(vb.), rhyme with *paid, affraid, saade* (= said),* *arayd,* and *manhed; visage* and *rage* with *knawlege; schame, name, blame,* with *thaim* (O.N. þeim), and *hame* (O.N. heim); *declare, spare, are* (vb.), with *mare* or *mair* (adj.), *debonaire, fare* or *fair* (adj.), *repar* (vb.), *aire* or *are* or *ere* or *eire* (adv.), *aire* (s.), *)ere, frere, hair,* &c.; *estate, debait,* &c., with *blait,* from O.N. bleyta, and *hate* (= hot, shortened in later Scottish into *het*) O.N. heitr, and *have* and *craif* (A.S. habban and crafan, but O.N. hefi and kref) with *laif* or *lave* or *laiffe* (O.N. leifar) and *resaif.* So in Barbour, who was contemporary with Chaucer, we find *slain,* which elsewhere and most frequently rhymes with *again,* as it might in Chaucer, rhyming repeatedly with *ane* = one (O.N. ein), *gane* = gone (O.N. geingit), and *tane* = taken; none of which rhymes would be admissible in Chaucer. Can it be that toward the close of Elizabeth's reign the probability, and afterwards the fact, of a Scottish succession to the throne, aided and accelerated, if it did not even cause, the change of pronunciation in England?

70 *The change in England did not take place through Stuart influence.* It seems very unlikely that mere court influence could have thinned down a full bold (aa) into (ee) or (ee) in the mouths of the sturdy Englishmen whom the early Stuarts ruled; and there are many indications of a rugged spirit of independence among the people that was quite prepared to resist court influence even in smaller matters than ship-money and episcopacy. Yet in Milton and Dryden such rhymes as *maid shade, fail ale pale, spare air bare, praise amaze, state wait,* are sufficiently common to suggest a

---

* No argument can be based on the mere spelling of the Scottish words, if Mr. Murray's view is correct that the *i* or *y* in these digraphs in Middle Scotch simply indicated the length of the vowel preceding. This view however still leaves it an open question what that preceding vowel itself was — whether (aa), (ee), or (ee) —in these words. But it will be observed that the argument in the text is based on the words themselves, irrespective of modes of writing. In Chaucer the past tense *made,* however spelt, never rhymed with *saide,* however spelt; and I should argue that the radical (a) in the former, and the radical (e) in the latter, sufficiently indicate an original distinction which in Middle Scotch has been blotted out.

suspicion that their not occurring more frequently is simply due to the fact that a word which is seeking a mate to rhyme with naturally looks among those of exactly the same form.* Still this is only a suspicion, and we may not tread on such thin ice with safety.

Here, however, are facts that may help us. Even before the close of the 16th century we find Smith, Hart, and Bullokar (like Gil only a little later) clearly distinguishing the *a* in *far, mark, allow, grammar, manner, half, after*, &c., from the *a*† in another large class of words—*blame, name, tame, same, bacon, capon, able, table, stable, declare, cradle, made, lady, make, take*, &c. &c. And yet all these orthoepists have a third quite distinct class of words, though they *now* are (e) words and would rhyme with the list last given. Such are *remain, say, great, plain, swear, their*, besides many more, which in modern times have changed (ee) or (ee) into (ii)—*receive, either, breathe, please*, &c.

71 *A had in some words, in Queen Elizabeth's time, a sound between (a) and (ee)* Since then *blame, name*, &c., had lost the sound of (aa), and had not yet acquired that of (ee), and yet were on the road to it; the conclusion seems unavoidable that in the time of Queen Elizabeth they had some intermediate (see § 28) sound. Most probably it was (æ), the sound of the *a* in *mat* or *man*, or (ææ), the same sound prolonged. Moreover Giles du Wes charges Englishmen in learning French to pronounce "your *e* almost as brode as ye pronounce your *a* in englysshe;" which points to the conclusion that it was the established habit of the English in Henry the Eighth's reign to sound their *a*, at least in many words, almost like *e*, that is probably (ææ). Palsgrave also (1530) clearly recognizes two *a*s in English, one of them the same

---

* Although in this 19th century *ail* and *ale*, *sow* and *sare*, &c., are beyond question, pronounced without the slightest distinction, yet in Byron's rhymes of *ee* words, setting aside the final *ee*, I find, in nearly seven instances out of eleven, the words are spelt alike; as, done in Tom Moore's. Sir Walter Scott, on the contrary, seems to have conspicuously exempted himself from such bondage, and to rhyme according to the verbal use.

† Written *a* by Hart, *a* by Smith and Gil, *a* by Bullokar.

as the French and Italian, the other different. It is therefore clearly not Scottish influence that commenced the change from (aa) to (æ) in these words, though it not improbably gave the (aa) its coup-de-grâce.

72. *Classes of 'A' words in Chaucer: some had (a).* But what of Chaucer, from whom Henry VIII. is distant more than a century? Answer, as in other cases,—distinguendum est.

Some words there are which in their earliest stage in the language had almost certainly (a), as certainly had (a) in the 16th century, and still have (a) in the 19th century. It is therefore scarcely questionable that they always have had that vowel in English. Such are *large, charge, bar, spar,* from the French *large, charge, barre,* Italian *sbarra,* and other such, including the interjection *a!* which takes *Emelya* with it (C.T. 1080), and therefore also probably the Latin termination in *omnia,* and the name of the vowel *A* itself (C.T. 161). In these words all the evidence is in favour of (a).

73. *Others had (A).* A second class, so far back as the orthoepists will carry us, was distinct from these, being written, or described as equal to, *aw* by Cooper (1685), *au* by Butler (1633), *â* by Gil (1621), *au* by Bullokar (1580), and *au* by Hart (1569). It includes *all, call, royal, several, dance, command,* &c.; many of which still retain the sound of (AA): that sound we shall probably be right in assigning to them in Chaucer's time also, though in so many of these words as are of Anglo-Saxon origin there is no difference in the mode of writing these and the class preceding.

It may be added that Butler expressly states[*] that in his time *a* before *l, nc,* and *nd* was sounded as *au;* and it is exactly in these words that the oldest and best MSS. of

---

[*] "*A* is in English, as in all other languages, the first vowel, and first letter of the Alphabet: the which, like *i* and *u*, hath two sounds: one when it is short, an other, when long: as in *man* and *mane, hat* and *hate*. And before *l* it is sounded like *au*: as in *also, palsi, fals, altar, alter, halter;* except *f, c, k, l,* or *m,* for then *al* hath the sound of *au*: before *ng,* for *ai,* as in *change, range, danger, stranger;* before *nc* like *au,* as in *chance, dance, france, lance;* and also before *nd,* as in *demand, command.*" P 5.

Chaucer seem to write almost indifferently -*ance* and -*aunce*, -*and* and -*aund*; more commonly with *au*. (I assume for the present, what I shall endeavour to prove further on, that *au* in Chaucer's time stood for (AA), as it does now.) Such words in Chaucer are *al, bal, calle, Malle, halle, schal, falle, wal, thral, general,* and other words of Latin derivation in -*al; penaunce, pitaunce, chaunce, meschaunce, daunce, daliaunce, remembrance, suffisaunce, countenaunce, plesaunce, comaunde,* &c. To these must be added *land, hand, stand,* and *strand,* which occasionally rhyme with *comaunde,* and show a sound other than (a) by their being not uncommonly spelt with *o*; and words in -*ant* (*servant, marchant, covenant,* &c.) are at least as frequently written with -*aunt*. Butler adds that *chaunge, straunge, daunger,* &c., in the North of England still retained the old pronunciation; and Chaucer's orthography indicates the same. Lastly the spelling of *ensample* also as *ensaumple,* and its rhyming with *temple,* suggest the French sound of the vowel in both of these. I take all of these words to have had (AA).

But words in -*ale* do not rhyme with those in -*al* or -*alle*, even when both have the final *e*. Such are *tale, pale, ale, male* (adj. and subst.), *dale, nightingale,* &c. I find, on running through over 6000 lines of the Canterbury Tales, twenty-two rhymes formed by these words with one another, and sixty of words in -*alle* with one another: only in three other instances does a word in -*ale* rhyme with one in -*alle*, and in each case it is *smale,* the pronunciation of which is thus seen to have been at that time unsettled.

The sound then of these -*ale* words seems to have been with (a) or (æ), but which of these, we will for the present leave undetermined. The repeated rhyme of *talys,* i.e. tales, with *Alys,* helps very little. *Alys,* now (æl´is), may have been (al´is) in Chaucer's time; or it may have been an inexact rhyme.

74. A third class had *a* in Chaucer, but not in Anglo-Saxon, and the modern pronunciation is various. The A.S. form has *œ*, which was probably (æ),*

* See § 117.

or, thinner still, *e*, i.e. (e). Such are *hadde*, A.S. hæfde; *was*, A.S. wæs; *black*, A.S. blæc; *bak*, A.S. bæc; *bladde*, A.S. blæd; *glas*, A.S. glæs; *bras*, A.S. bræs; *skathe*, A.S. sceðan; *Bathe*, A.S. bæð; *hath*, A.S. hæfð. Some of these are now pronounced with (a), some with (æ), some with (A), some with (ee). The 16th century writers do not assist us, as they do not distinguish short (a) from short (æ); but as the majority had apparently the same sound in A.S. as in modern English, it is reasonable to conclude that they have had the same sound during the whole interval. Some words of French derivation go with these—*cas*, *pas* (subst.), *solas*, *alas*, &c. rhyming with *bras* and *was*, for instance; so that we must suppose them also to have assumed this peculiarly English vowel. Then these words will be (bræs), (glæs), (alæs), (hæth), (hæd), (blæk), (pæs), just as at present; and (solæs), (Bæth) or (Bææth),* (wæs), (cæs) (skæth), (spræd), (spæk), contrary to present use.

It is notable however that the verbs *pace* and *solace*, together with *space*, *grace*, *face*, *place*, *embrace*, *manace*, *Trace* (i.e. Thrace), *purchace*, of French derivation, and *lasse* and *asse* from the A.S. *læssa* and *assa*, refuse to rhyme with *gras*, *bras*, &c. The final *e* however sufficiently accounts for this.

75. *A fourth class had a longer (æ) or (ææ).* But there yet remain others chiefly of French origin in -*age*, -*able*, -*ame*, -*ate*, &c., as to which, as well as those in -*ale* and -*ace* already referred to, and numerous English words in -*are*, -*ake*, &c., the imperfect evidence seems to leave it doubtful whether (æ) or (a) was the pronunciation in Chaucer's age. But though the problem is difficult, a faint ray of light seems to fall on it from the Ormulum. Assuming that *make*,

---

* It is not easy in the case of several of these words to determine whether the vowel is long or short, and therefore whether (æ) or (ææ) is the right symbol. It is certain that few or perhaps no English speakers pronounce *ass*, *glass*, *grass*, *pass* with as short a vowel as that in the first syllable of *astronomical*, and yet they do not so prolong the sound as a Somersetshire peasant in naming *Bath*. We have in fact, as Mr. Melville Bell and others have pointed out, various degrees of length of our vowels, minute differences of quantity as well as quality in different words.

from the A.S. *macian*, and *take*, from the O.N. *taka*, were in their earliest forms sounded with (aa), we find that in Ormin's time they had undergone a change, at least in the imperatives, which he writes *macc* and *tacc*. This doubled consonant is Ormin's mode of indicating a short preceding vowel; and these imperatives in this form have the same vowel as that of *annd*, *att*, *bacc*, *brass*, *chappmenn*, &c. It is true, Ormin's short *a*, like his long one, may have stood for more sounds than one; so that before *r*, as in *arrke*, *arrmess* (i.e. arms), *arrt*, the vowel may have been the short (a); but the point that I call attention to is the fact that the *a* in *macc* and *tacc* has been shortened, and before the guttural tenuis it is more likely, as in the other instances, that the sound was (æ). And it may be so that the very thing which Ormin intended by his *ă* (sic) was (ææ); for six out of the eight words which he so writes—the other two do not occur in Chaucer—are among the very words which we are discussing. They are, *dăle*, *hătenn* (also hatenn), *lăte* (also late), *năme* (also name), *tăkenn*, and *tăle* (also tale). And we are not at all bound to assume that the ˘ signified what we now use it to signify, especially as Ormin had another mode of showing the short vowel. At any rate this *ă* indicates some other sound than the *a* of *afell* (Icel. afl), *afledd*, *abidenn*, *abufenn*, *abutenn*, *adl*, *anig*, &c.,*—in other words, some *change*; and since four of these words have forms in *a* also, the change itself seems to have been incomplete, and the pronunciation unsettled when Ormin wrote. If then English words had (aa) in Anglo-Saxon, but at least since the seventeenth century have had (ee), and there are even as soon as the early part of the thirteenth century signs of an incipient change; it is but reasonable to suppose that that change was somewhat advanced when Chaucer wrote, a century and a half later. And if we may so conclude for English words, it is highly probable

---

* Very many of Ormin's *a* words, as *af*, *or*, *nn*, *on*, *gatt*, *mann*, *off*, were from A.S. words with *a*, and I therefore believe them to have been sounded with (aa).

that French words too (as we have just seen *cas, pas, solas*, &c., made to rhyme with *glas* and *bras*) would be drawn into the same vortex of now prevailing English sound. I infer that (blææm) or (blæænu), (fææs) or (fæærsu, smææl), (træk), (estæært), (vizææ̆dzh) or (vizææ̆dzhu), (sææv) or (sæævu), &c., were Chaucer's sounds.

And this is confirmed by the fact that these words with the long (or at least longer) vowel rhyme now and then with others with the short one. *Blade* rhymes both with *hadde* and with *panade; spake* rhymes with *wake*, as well as with *bak, blak*, and *demoniac; pace* (vb.) with *lasse*, A.S. læssa, as well as with *space, grace*, &c. This may be best explained by supposing that while in the one set of rhymes (as *blade* and *panade*) the *quantity* of the vowels was the same, the *quality* was the same in the other (as *blade* and *hadde*).

76 *A in Chaucer not made (A by a w preceding.* Finally, whether the vowel was long or short, it was not affected as in modern English by a *w* preceding: *wan* rhymed with *man, swau* with *Jovinian; warm* with *arm, quarte* with *parte, what* with *sat*, and so on. So it is in the Devonshire dialect to this day. I have a lively recollection of having heard (ɔs mɔs wæ˞rm 'n)* for "We must beat him," namely the dog; and (wæd *i zee*) for "What do you say?" is perfectly common.+

77 *Mr. Ellis makes Chaucer's a always (a).* It is certainly a singular instance of Mr. Ellis's want of discrimination, that he should make the short *a* in Chaucer always (a), forgetting that it includes the A.S. *æ* as well as *a*, and the modern (æ) as well as (a). Many of Chaucer's words in *a* were spelt with *æ* in A.S.—æt, þæt, hæfð, æsp, (aspen), æsc, glæs, tæppestre, &c.—and sounded as Mr. Ellis (rightly, I think) supposes, with (æ), in the Anglo-Saxon period, and they are sounded with the same sound now: yet they had (a) in Chaucer! This is precisely the kind of "interregnum" which Mr. Ellis elsewhere protests against in somewhat felicitous phrase. Is it in fact in the slightest degree

---

* (Warm) is also used.

+ And compare the modern Scotch pronunciation of *wash* as (wɑsh).

probable that *tapster* would be (tæp·estre) in A.S., turn into (tapsteer) in the fourteenth century, and go back to (tæp·stɹ) in these later centuries? Yet such strange confusion must result if an investigator allows himself to be misled by the notion that 'the orthography [sufficiently] shows the sound.' Surely it is vastly more probable that though the influence of the Norman Conquest so far modified the *mode of writing* of our forefathers as to cause *æ* with other letters to be disused, yet the *mode of speaking* in the utterance of common words would remain the same, and the distinction between (a) and (æ), though blotted out of the *written* language, would yet survive in the *spoken* language, as beyond question it does for the most part to this day.

Mr. Ellis's inconsistency is all the more remarkable as he supposes some of the words which had (æ) in A.S. and assumed the broader (a) in Chaucer to have actually deviated into a thinner sound in the interval. According to his view * our word that was in the A.S. times (thæt), in Henry II.'s time it shrunk up into (dhet), in Chaucer's time it expanded again into (dhat), and in this nineteenth century—and indeed for more than two centuries now—has returned to its original sound, at least as to the vowel.

We pass on now to another class of words, those which

78 In a large number of 'E' words tradition fixes the sound as (ii). are written with *e*, which Mr. Ellis affirms was (e), as it still is (when followed by *r*) in *ere, were, where, there.*

Now there are certain words to which our provincial dialects agree in assigning the sound of (ii), and which even Mr. Ellis acknowledges to have been so sounded for at least three centuries. Here are some of them: *he, she, me, thee, we, ye, the, be, bee, see, flee, tree, three, free, knee, fleece, smeeth, feed, breed, need, heed, bleed, meed, speed, reed, weed, lief, week, reek, seek, feel, heel, keel, wheel, field, green, queen, thirteen, fourteen,* &c., *keen, ween, keep, sheep, deep, weep, steep, beer, here, deer, geese, priest, meet, greet, fleet, sheet, feet, sweet, beet, teeth, seethe.* I can find no trace that any one of these words is ever pronounced with (ee) in the western

* See pp. 535, 593, 710, 65.

dialects or any other. The tradition is uniform with regard to them, and they all are spelt in Early and Modern English with *e* or *ee*, three only with *ie*. In Anglo-Saxon they are also spelt with *é* or *eó*; in most cases with the accent. I urge then that, unless there be any insuperable objection, tradition fixes the pronunciation of these words; and that the written *é* in A.S. is the symbol of the same sound as the *ee* in Modern English.

80 *Pronunciation of A.S. eá and eó.* Do I then suppose that *é* and *eó* were pronounced alike in the time of King Alfred? Not quite alike, but I believe that in the diphthongs *eá* and *eó* the accent, though written on the second vowel (as we write the accent in Greek), belonged partly or exclusively to the first, the second vowel being the weaker one. This is rendered probable by the fact that the *ó* in these words is so easily abraded. (I shall return to this subject by-and-by.) "In the Ormulum," Dr. Morris tells us, "*eo* occurs, but with the sound of *e*, and *ea* in Genesis and Exodus is written for *e*." I suspect, however, not the pure (ii) in either case. Mr. Sweet in a recent paper has spoken of *l* as commonly preceded by a pure vowel. In Devonshire it is not so: the A.S. ceól, hweól, seem to be preserved with little change — perhaps none — in the Dev. (kiiəl), (whiiəl); and *school* in Dev. is (skœəl).*

80 *Derivation of she.* And here I may observe that I cannot accept Mr. Ellis's derivation of our pronoun *she*. He takes it from *heó*, the A.S. fem. of *he*. I take it from *seó*, fem. of *se* or *þat*. In *seó*, *shoe*, the *e* seems to be a mere orthographical expedient to indicate the pronunciation of the *se* as the modern *sh*, and the *ó*, as I contend, is (uu); so that the word was pronounced 1000 years ago as

---

* Not (skyyl). I am a Devonshire man, and know most parts of Devonshire pretty well. I have also lived in France, and know French well. And I affirm that I have never heard the pure French *u* in the Dev. dialect. It is much more nearly the Fr. *eu* or *eû* that is there substituted for (uu). (Mr. Ellis tells one he has heard both sounds; I have not. Prince Louis Lucien Bonaparte, certainly a most competent judge, tells me that to his ear the sound is between the Fr. *u* and *eu*.)

it is now. In like manner the *e* is a mere orthographical expedient in sceáwian, sceaft, sceamu, scearp, &c.; and in gearu, geára, geard, geoc (which was *yŏk* in Chaucer's time), geond, geógu%, &c. *In seó* on the contrary (as in geár, sceáf, sceóp, &c.), the *e* is not a mere orthographical expedient, but the principal part of the diphthong, the word having been, as I suppose, pronounced (siiu). Then the *s*, as commonly when followed by (i) and another vowel (e.g. nation, ocean, sure, sugar; vision, pleasure, &c.), becomes *sh*.* Finally, as in a multitude of other instances, the *o* is abraded, and the *e* remains; though sometimes the *o* had more vitality and overpowered the *e*, so that *sho* resulted. Compare *sceótan* as the original of the O.E. *shete* as well as the modern *shoot*; and *yeoman* as pronounced by Chaucer and by Ben Jonson (jiimæn), and as now pronounced. That *float* has prevailed over Chaucer's *fleten* may be ascribed to the influence of the French *flotter* on the side of *flotian* as against *fleótan*; for there were both these forms in A.S.

81. **The broad sound of *e* as (ee) in the Western dialects only partial: the line drawn.** But to return. There are many *e* words in which modern provincial usage is divided even within the limits of one and the same dialect. Thus in Devonshire we have both *cheek* and *chayke* (tsheeïk), *leech* and *laych*, *meal* (miil)—from the mill—and *mayl*, *clean* and *clayn*, *flea* or *vlea* and *vlay*, *sea* and *say*, *heap* and *hayp*, *read* and *rayd*, *rear* and *rayr*, *meat* and *mayt*; and just so in Anglo-Saxon most of these same words appear in more forms than one—léce, lǽce, méte, mǽte, clén, clǽn, réran, rǽran, &c. But in the list of words I have above quoted—*he, me, keep, teeth,* &c.—I can find no trace of such diversity of pronunciation either now or formerly. A Devonshire countryman—and I affirm it not merely from my own knowledge, but after inquiry from others, and after having carefully searched Nathan Hogg's

---

* Instances of this change are so numerous that I cannot believe with Mr. Murray (who also derives *she* from *seó*, p. 120) that this form arose in the Northern dialect and then "was adopted also into the Midland and Southern dialects."

Poems and Mrs. Gwatkin's Devonshire Dialogue—may talk of going "to *say*" for "to sea," but he will never pronounce the verb *see* as *say*, nor *knee* as *nay*, *teeth* as *tayth*, and so on. There are on the other hand cases in which the A.S. word had an *e* which in some counties is now (ee) or (εε), as *crayp* (though *creep* is more common) from *creópan*; *baym* from *beám* or *beóm* in Sussex and some parts of Cornwall, though (biim) or (biiəm) is the pronunciation elsewhere. But such words are far from numerous. Almost all the words which in A.S. had *é*, and which survive in modern English, have the sound of (ii) or (*ii*).

82 *Evidence for (ii) from Dutch and German.* Moreover the Dutch and German forms of many of these words point to the same conclusion as the English dialects, as will be seen from the following list :—

Engl.	Du.	Germ.
see	zien	(sehen)
flee	vlieden	fliehen
knee	knie	knie
reed	riet	Rieth
lief	lief	lieb
wheel	wiel	———
heel	hiel	Hiel
keel	kiel	Kiel
-teen	-tien	(-zehn)
deep	diep	tief
shete (= shoot)	schieten	schiessen
flete (= float)	vlieten	fliessen
beer	bier	Bier
deer	dier	Thier
here	hier	hier
reek	rieken	riechen
fleece	vlies	Vliess
seethe	zieden	sieden

83 *On a sound near (ii) is found in the German, Dutch, &c., congeners of English 'e' words.* Then again in many instances where the German congener of an English word with (i) does not itself contain (i), it has a sound close akin to (i), but very remote from (e). Thus:

the natural order of the vowel sounds, as is now admitted, is

(i) (e) (a) (A) (o) (u) (y);

and the extremes meet in some way that has not yet, so far as I know, been explained,* so that our *Miller* and the German *Müller* are pronounced almost alike: the one sound passes with great facility into the other. And in the words referred to, while the English word has the first sound (i) of the above natural series, its congeners are furnished from the other end of the series with (y) or even (u), the latter especially in Dutch. Thus hüten (Du. hoeden, Kil.) *heed*, kühn (Du. koen) = *keen*, grün (Du. groen) = *green*, süss (Du. zoet) = *sweet*, grüssen (Du. groeten) = *greet*, fühlen (Du. voelen) *feel*, Füsse (Du. voeten) = *feet*, &c.

In like manner it may be argued that the congeners in other languages of many of the words which Mr. Ellis would pronounce with (e), are all found vowelled from the other end of the system. Thus *knee* has for kinsmen the Greek γόνυ (with γνύξ, πρόχνυ, ἰγνύα), Lat. *genu*, Skt. *jânu*, Zend *zenu*, M.G. *kniu*. In O.N. alone is there any (e), but then accompanied by (i), *hné* being pronounced, and sometimes written, *hnie* (hniee). Indeed scarcely any congeners can be found with (e) for any of the words above given (§ 78), except only *sehen* and *-zehn* given in the last list.

The conclusion to which I am forced by this evidence from various sources—confirmed as it is to a certain extent by the testimony of Ben Jonson for the 17th century, and Palsgrave for the 16th (see § 86—is that all these words have been sounded with (ii) in every age of our language, the 14th century of course included. And with these go many other words whose final syllable has a long *e* for its vowel, as the rhymes of the poets prove beyond all doubt.

84. *EA words had ... for (ee); they never rhymed with E words.* But Mr. Ellis finds reasons for believing—and I have arrived at the same conclusion—that most, or perhaps all, of the words which in Chaucer's time were spelt with a simple *e*, but which two centuries later were spelt with *ea*, were at this later period

* I am told that Mr. Melville Bell has thrown light on this.

pronounced with (*ee*) or (ee), while those that continued to be spelt with *e* or *ee* were at that later time pronounced with (ii). Such words are *sea, flea, each, teach, preach, reach, beast, feast, read, lead* (vb.), *mead, sheaf, leaf, weak, speak, meal, deal, beam, dream, stream, bean, mean, lean, clean, heap, rear, tear* (s.), *tear* (vb.), *eat, heat, meat, wheat, heath, wreath, leave, weave, please, ease, tease release, cease.* (I have not had time to make a complete list; though I should like to have done so, for such inquiries are, to a much greater extent than Mr. Ellis seems to suspect, inquiries about individual words.) All of these are often—perhaps most commonly—pronounced in the western counties with (*ee*)—*say, vlay, aych, taych,* and so on; but almost all of them (though *flea* has the same form in A.S.) are derived either from A.S. words with *é* or *æ* (? *ǽ*), or from O.N. words with *ei*, or from French words with some modification of (e). These words therefore having been formerly pronounced with (*ee*) or (ee)—*rǽdan, tǽcan, hǽp, veikr, prescher, aise,* &c.—but being now pronounced with (ii), have at some time or other undergone a change; and I agree with Mr. Ellis that the change (at least in our southern dialects) has taken place later than the middle of the 17th century. In Ben Jonson the words *deem, seem, esteem, redeem,* rhyme with one another, but do not once in all his poems rhyme with *dream, stream, moonbeam; feel, steel, eel, heel, wheel,* do not once rhyme with *real, seal, steal, weal, deal* (portion), *deal* (board), *meal, heal, conceal, reveal, zeal; geese, piece, Greece, fleece,* do not once rhyme with *peace, increase, cease, release; deep, sleep, weep, keep, peep, steep, creep, sheep,* not once with *cheap, reap, heap, leap;* and so on. In Spenser, so far as I have examined, the same distinction is observed, though I have found *speed* once rhyming with *dread,* and *peer* with *ear,* as occasional imperfect rhymes must be expected.* I have also examined the whole of Sir Philip Sidney's rhymes, and all of Heywood's

---

* But as to *peer, ear,* if the latter was (eer), we may remember that the former is from the French *pair,* and Spenser may possibly have used the word with the ancient sound, spelling notwithstanding.

rhymes in his Proverbs and Epigrams (1562), and with like result.

85 *Nor do these words rhyme in Chaucer, though spelt alike.* But now I must recall attention to the remark I made at starting as to the importance of not confounding written language with the spoken, which alone is language proper. It is the spoken language with which we are primarily concerned; and Mr. Ellis has been seriously misled through his attending too exclusively to the written symbols of language. I shall doubtless astonish him when I assert, and demonstrate, that *the very same distinction* that exists between these classes of words in Ben Jonson, Spenser, Sir Philip Sidney, Heywood, and other poets of that age, *exists also in Chaucer, clearly and strongly marked, though disguised by the spelling.* What Mr. Ellis, justly for the most part, calls an innovation, namely the spelling of words of the latter class with *ea*, in Chaucer's time was yet unknown. But for all that the words, though spelt alike, were not spoken alike. The "so sharp distinction" which Mr. Ellis imagines (p. 242) between the English of Chaucer and that of Spenser does not exist. This must be looked at more in detail.

86 *Final e in Chaucer was (ii).* There is not indeed in the case of the accented final *e* any distinction between (ii) and (ee) words,—I assume for the moment that the two classes may be correctly thus designated—; and I shall endeavour to prove that all belong to the former class. The only word which for reasons already indicated we might expect to find pronounced with (ee) is the noun *sea*, in the Devonshire dialect *say*. But it had in A.S. not only the form *sǽ*, but also *se* (*sé*?) and *seo* (Bosw.); and Chaucer seems to have retained only these. He uses the word rhyming with *he, see, tree*, &c.

Now Ben Jonson lays down the rule that "When *e* is the last letter, and soundeth, the sound is sharp, as in the French *i*." In Palsgrave, a century earlier, we do not find this stated as a rule, nor have we a right to expect it; but all the examples he gives are in accordance with it—*bee es., fee*, and also "dyvers other pronownes ending in *e*, as *we, me, the, he, she,* and suche lyke." All of these he sounds like the French or Italian *i*. But was the usage the same in Chaucer's time? I claim the right to affirm, on the ground of the *vis inertiæ* of language (see §§ 6 to 9), that it was the same, unless the contrary can be proved; and the only arguments to prove the contrary are, first, the pure assumption—and a highly improbable one too—that in common English speech foreign words (such as the Latin *benedicite,* and the French *magesté, degré,* &c.) were *not* anglicized; and secondly, the use of one actual French word.

And this one French word, pardé—to deal with it first—
87   Pardé.   in fact only confirms my conclusion, if at least the final *i* in French was sometimes sounded (i) (see § 13). For *pardi* is the common form in French, as used by Voltaire (quoted by Littré) and at the present day. Chaucer uses the word both as *pardé* and *perdy.* Spenser and Shakspeare also use the latter form, Shakspeare making it rhyme with *fly.* I suspect it had both sounds in French (ii) and (əi). (If *pardé* existed in French in Chaucer's time—but I cannot find it, though I do find *dé* God—we must simply consider the pronunciation as anglicized.)

And as to anglicized pronunciation, even if we did not
88   Tendency to anglicize foreign words.   find mention in Chaucer of French spoken "After the scole of Stratford atte Bowe," we might expect such anglicizing from the tendency continually exemplified around us to pronounce foreign words in the easiest manner. Not only do we hear *Mounseer* for *Monsieur,* and (sendziindiieeks) for *St. Jean d'Acre;* but witness the recognised pronunciation of *chagrin, bombazine, chenille, patty, bergamot,* and of military terms as *enfilade, calibre,* &c., and of geographical names as *Mexico, Saragossa, Sherry, Canton, Sedan, Paris,* &c. Especially might we look for such modifications of foreign sounds in an age when there was hardly any travelling, and when there was therefore no motive for preserving them with exactness.

A curious instance of this anglicizing is found in the

Rom. of the Rose (p. 164 in Bell's edition), where *parcuere*, i.e. par cœur, is made to rhyme with *lere*. The latter is probably in this case an (ee) word (as we shall presently find that it is, very exceptionally), but even then the vowel is sufficiently remote from the French *cuer*, *coer*, or *queur*, all of which I believe to have been merely different modes of representing the same sound as *cœur* represents.*

I have therefore not the slightest difficulty in believing that *mageste*, *equite*, and such like words, when adopted into English, assumed the common English pronunciation of the final *e*, i.e. (ii) or (*i*).

89 *Latin no exception to the rule.* As to Latin however Mr. Ellis seems to think himself warranted in assuming that the vowels were sounded in England in the continental mode; nor is he alone in supposing that the priesthood in this island had a traditional pronunciation of ecclesiastical Latin in which an approximation to the Italian pronunciation was maintained.† So far as I can learn, this notion is simply a delusion. Two learned Catholic Doctors of my acquaintance, one the president of St. —— 's College, and the other the Prior of ——, inform me that such traditional pronunciation has no existence. The late Cardinal Wiseman endeavoured with considerable success to introduce the Italian pronunciation of Latin among English priests, but before his time there prevailed — and still largely prevails — a mongrel pronunciation, half French half English. The French element was due to the dispersion of the priests at the time of the Persecution (what we call the Reformation), when many of them took refuge in St. Omer and other places in France; but prior to the Persecution there was only *the English pronunciation* of Latin in this country. I have not had the opportunity of referring to

---

* In Stanza xxii. of the Chanson de Roland we find several words with *e* in assonance with *lere* (plur. of *jeu* = fiefs), as well as *als* = yeux, while one of these *ee* words, *essct* = il faut, is found in Matzner's Altfr. Lieder, xxxiv. 26, in the form *e tuet*.

† Thus Mr. Payne says: "The assumption with which I commence is that the literary pronunciation of Church Latin in the thirteenth century was a tradition of ages," p. 360.

books in corroboration of these statements, and therefore content myself with quoting as my authority men of learning who speak with confidence as on a matter with which they are familiarly acquainted. Precisely what "the English pronunciation" of Latin was, it may be hard to say; but at any rate the assumption that the final vowel of *benedicite* was sounded in the French or Italian manner cannot for a moment be admitted as a trustworthy premiss pointing towards Mr. Ellis's conclusion. The "English pronunciation" was far more probably just what it is now.

Then we notice that three classes of words with vowel terminations have been borrowed from French into English, all of which in the 19th century commonly end in (i), but which in the 14th century had different terminations, as exemplified in *enemi* (enemǝi)—I take Palsgrave's authority, though two centuries later, for its pronunciation,—*cheminee* (tsheminecǝ), and *majesté* (madzheste), in modern English (enem*i*), (tsh*i*mn*i*), (madzhest*i*). Now the first two of these classes gave no trouble to the English ear or tongue, which were already familiar with similar terminations; and so we readily get (remedǝi), (tsh*i*vǝlrǝi), (ostelrǝi), &c., and—with a slight modification of the (ee-ǝ)—(tsh*i*mnee), (valee), (dzhǝurnee), (galee), &c.; but the third class ended in a sound, the short pure (e), which, as a final, was quite strange to English organs both of hearing and of speech. Hence, as was most natural, the nearest English sound, (i) or (*i*), was substituted; and in consequence we have *charite* (tshar*i*t*i*), *jolyte* (dzhol*i*t*i*), *degre, destine, secre, prive, livere*, as well as *Galile, Nineve, Canace, benedicite*, all rhyming habitually and invariably with *me, we, he, she, thee, knee, three, tree*, &c.*

90 Three classes of words now terminating in (i), formerly distinct.

91 Words in *ere*, part with (ii), part with (ee): the two classes quite distinct.

I pass on to words in –*ere*, –*eere*, &c., all of which Mr. Ellis would pronounce indiscriminately with (eer). In fact there are two distinct classes here. I have collected, I believe, *all* the rhymes with this written termination throughout the

---

* *Be, nycete*, has been spoken of as a false rhyme: it is rather a case of false spelling: it should be *nycete*.

§ 91]   TWO DISTINCT CLASSES OF 'E' WORDS.   67

Canterbury Tales, and with the following results. The words *here** (vb.), *here* (adv.), *dere* (adj.), *deer* (s.), *chere*, *clere*, *fere* (= companion), *frere*, *appere*, and some others, rhyme with one another habitually. Again, the adverbs *there* and *where*, *were* (from *be*), *bere* (vb.), *bere* (s., = ursus), *gere*, *spere*, *tere* (s.)—now (giiɹ), (spiiɹ), and (tiiɹ),—*here* (= crinis), *cere* (s.), *ere* (vb.), *ere* (adv.), and others, rhyme with one another habitually. But these two classes do not rhyme with one another—or *very* rarely : I will give the exact figures presently. With the former class, which occasionally and exceptionally are written with *-iere*, all words derived from French originals in *-ier* and *-iere* rhyme habitually, such as *bachiler*, *tapisser*, *ryvere*, *manere*, *matere*, &c. On the other hand the A.S. terminations *-ere* and *-stere* belong to what for the present and for distinction sake we may call the (ee) class. Only in the words *year*, which had in A.S. the two forms *gér* and *geár*, and *bier*, an (ee) word in A.S., but an (ii) word in Palsgrave's time, is any hesitancy of pronunciation to be discerned. These two words therefore I set aside. Then here are the lists, the numbers indicating the exceptions—the halting rhymes or (perhaps more probably) unsettled pronunciation. First the (ii) class: *here* (vb.), 58-0; *here* (adv.), 40-0; *clere* and *Chauntielere*, 19-0; *chiere*, 51-0; *dere* (adj.), 81-2;† *in fere*, 9-0; *bachiler*, *tapicer*, &c., 31-0; *manere*, *rivere*, &c., 113-1; *nere* (adv.), 6-0; *peer*, 7-0; *appiere*, 4-0; *deer* (s.), 3-0; *frere*, 23-1; *leere* (s., which is the old Dutch *lier*, cheek), 2-0; *lere* (vb. = learn), 15-1; but *year*, 31-8; *bier*, 8-4. With these are found *paupere* (whatever that may mean, l. 12690), once; *stere* (steersman), twice; *pikerbeer*, once; *bere*, pret. of *bear*

* As to the spelling of these words, so unsettled in the age of Chaucer, and in the various MSS., I have taken at haphazard the form which has first caught my eye.

† To make the meaning of these figures clearer, I may explain that in the Cant. Ta. the adj. *dere* is found in eighty-one distichs in all; that in seventy-nine of these it rhymes with (ii) words, and only in two cases, which are specified lower down, does it rhyme with (ee) words. *Chere* is found in twenty-one distichs, rhyming exclusively with (ii) words.

(A.S. ber) twice;* *soper*, three times.† The (ee) class consists of these words: *were* (pret. of *be*), 32–2; *there*, 24–0; *where*, 10–0; *were* (= Lat. gerere), 3–0; *teere* (s.), 16–0; *swere* (vb.), 8–0; *bere* (vb.), 8–0; *bere* (s. = ursus), 6–1; *here* (= hair), 10–0; *ere* (s. = ear), 14–0; *ere* (adv.), 2–0; *fere* (= timor), 6–0; *gere*, 8–1; *her* (pron.) 8–0; *spere*‡ (s. = hasta), 7–0. With these are the A.S. *mellere, tapstere*, &c., with *Finistere, mere* (= mare), *were* (= defend), *dere* (= injure), *shere* (s. = shear-s), *tere* (vb.), *answere, enquere*, and *requere*. The exceptions out of a total of 659 rhymes, *year* and *bier* being set aside, are only the following nine. *Dere* (adj.) rhymes once with *were* (from be), and once with *werre* (= war). *Frere* (= friar), rhymes once with *mere*. *Matere* rhymes once with *gramere*, which I assume to be an (e) word, Fr. *grammaire*. *Bere* (s.) rhymes once with *stere* (= ox), A.S. steor, which I assume to be an (i) word. *Gear* rhymes once with *brere*, A.S. brér, Old Norman *briere*. *Requere* rhymes once with *lere* (s.) And lastly *clear* and *Chaunticlere* rhyme once each with *powere*, which I assume to be an (e) word from its French form *pooir, puer, poeir, poueir*, which were all probably (poweer), and from its Scottish form *poware*. But in examining these words in -*ere*, I refer of course to the spoken words, regardless of varieties of spelling. The first of the above classes has eight varieties: *er, ere, eer, eere, ire, ier, iere*, and *yere* (as in *prayere*, a Picard corruption of Prov. *preguiera* or some such earlier form).

92 French words in -*ier* or -*iere* belong to the (ii) class. A list of the French words in *ier* or *iere* above alluded to which Chaucer uses—an imperfect list I fear—is the following, some, which are bracketed, being guessed from analogy, though most are to be found in the dictionaries: (annuelier),

---

* This preterit *bere* also rhymes with *bachelere* in Rom. of the Rose, p. 55 (Bell's edn.), but in p. 63 it rhymes with *there*.

† Which Mr. Payne also (p. 441) quotes as rhyming with *clere* in "Land of Cockayne."

‡ *Spere* = sphere is an (ii) word, rhyming with *dere, manere*, and *clere* in Tr. and Cr., bk. v.

antiphonier, archier, bachelier, bouclier, charpentier, collier, (corniculier), coursier,* daungier, escolier, escuyer, (fermerier), forestier, gauffrier,† Gaultier, heronier, hostelier, (labourier), marinier, messagier, officier, (pardonnier), particulier, premier, rosier, seculier, (soupier?), tavernier, vergier, (volupier);— briere, chambriere, corniere, derriere, maniere, matiere, panthiere,‡ priere, riviere. The termination *-ier* is so common in Old French that Cotgrave has in one place no fewer than six such words in two consecutive pages—*coursier, courtier, coustellier, coustillier, coustumier, and cousturier.* And that there might be a form *labourier* side by side with *laboureur* is shown by the coexistent *fourmagier* and *fourmageur*, *tuillier* and *tuileur*, &c. As to the pronunciation of this termination as (iir) in the English forms of these words, we still preserve it in *cashier* (O. Fr. caissier), *grenadier, engineer*, (O. Fr. enginier), *croupier, cuirassier, arrears,* &c.; while the sound is the same in the Dutch *Kassier, officier, griffier, granadier,* &c., and in the German *Offizier, Granatier,* &c.

93 *Pronunciation and meaning of Chaucer's name.* To the same class belongs the name of Chaucer, or Chaucere (Man of Lawes Tale, Headlink, l. 47, Petw. MS.), himself. I cannot indeed find in the dictionaries the form *chaussier*, but it would be quite regularly formed from *chausses*, as *chaussetier* from *chauss-*

---

* In the Flower and the Leaf occurs the strangely loose rhyme of *weare* (=wore), *were, corsere;* but Mr. Furnivall has shown good reasons for believing this poem not to be a genuine production of Chaucer. See *Athenæum* for July 13th, 1872.

† This or *goffrier* must have been the French form which *wafrer* represents in Cant. Ta. 13804, one of the two lines which Mr. Wright brackets. The passage stands thus:

    And right anoon ther come tombesteris
    [Fetis and smale, and yonge fruitesteres,
    Singers with harpes, baudes, wafereres,]
    Which that ben verray develes officeres.

The omission would give a false rhyme of Fr. *-ere* (iir) with A.S. *-ere* (eer) *tombesteris* with *officeres*. In other words, if established on MS. authority, it would add one to my nine bad rhymes mentioned above. [This note was written long before the publication of the Six-Text Chaucer, in which the lines are found in every one of the texts].

‡ *Panter* in Rom. of the Rose, p. 66 (Bell's edition).

ettes, while the modern equivalent *hosier* has preserved the same brief form. It is an idle dream indeed that the name was ever sounded *more semi-Germanico*, as (khauk.ɹ).

94 *Influence of final e in -iere words.* The influence of the final *e* in these rhymes I have no time fully to discuss; suffice to say that it prevents the Fr. *-iere* words from ever rhyming with the Fr. *ier* words (except, perhaps only, *bacheler* with *ryver* l. 6466, and *archers* with *corners* in Rom. of the Rose, p. 143), though both rhyme almost indifferently with *here* (vb.), *here* (adv.), &c. But if I may here recall attention to the theory which I have ventured elsewhere* to advance, that 'whenever the final *e* represents a final *syllable* in Anglo-Saxon [or old French], it *may*—not *must*—be sounded, and never otherwise;' I would suggest that when *manere* rhymes with the verb *here*, they possibly both sounded the final *e*; but if with the adverb *here*, which never had the final *e* (except as a mere orthographical expedient to indicate the length of the root vowel: A.S. hér, Icel. hèr, Du. hier, Ger. hier, Pl. D. hier, M. G. her), *manere* also dropped it; while there was felt to be an incongruity in rhyming two words both of French origin, such as *archere* (O. Fr. archier) and *rivere* (O. Fr. riviere), and pronouncing one accurately, while taking a liberty with the termination of the other.

95 *Words in -ene fall into two distinct classes.* Let us proceed to *-ene*; and for a change let us examine some of Chaucer's other poems. Well, in the Troilus and Cryseyde, Chaucer's Dreme, Chaucer's A. B. C., The Boke of the Duchesse, and one or two minor pieces, I have noted 125 rhymes, of which 100 are furnished by what seem to be (ii) words—*seene* (inf.), *sene* or *y-sene* (part.), *tene* (vexation), *shene*, *demene* (demeanour), *strene*, *wene* (think), *Polixene*—anglicized, it will be observed,—*qwene*, *grene*, *kene*, *bitwene*, *knene* (pl. of *knee*), *ben* (are), *ben* (inf.), *bene* (part.), *been* bees, *eene* (eyes, Sc. e'en, in four passages: elsewhere we have once *yen* rhyming with *crien*, *susteene*, *conteene*, *evene* (evening) and *fiftene*. The other 25 are made by *tene* (ta'en, and

* See below, § 118.

five other words which in the West of England are now sounded with *ayn* (*een*)—*mene* (s. = means, O. Fr. meyn or meen), *bene* (s. = bean), *lene* (adj.), *mene* (vb.), and *clene*. Now the notable fact is that in these poems of Chaucer these six words only twice* rhyme with the former class, namely *mene* twice with *wene;* but Chaucer then uses *mene* in the special sense of *to moan*. This obviously suggests a doubt whether our etymologists are right in making *mene* = mean and *mene* = moan the same word. I cannot believe they are the same. I suspect rather that at least to Chaucer's own apprehension the word was totally unconnected with *mind*, &c., and simply one of the imitative class, conveying the idea of a thin, feeble, plaintive cry, like *squeak*, *squeal*, and the old *peep*, rather than of anything approaching a groan.

The inf. *sleen* rhymes with *Egipcienc*, which, judging from the analogy of *Polixene*, must have had (ii), and so *sle* rhymes with *he;* but *sleth* occurs rhyming with *deth*, and the modern form is *slay:* usage as to this word was perhaps unsettled, as in many words now-a-days.

96 *Two distinct classes of words in -eme.* I have examined almost or quite the whole of Chaucer's poems for some other terminations. In -*eme* we have *seme, deme, queme, diademe*—and διάδημα we know has been pronounced for centuries with η (ii), —rhyming repeatedly with one another, but not once —notwithstanding that Mr. Ellis would make them all (eem) alike—with *dreme, reme* (= realm), rood-*beme*, sunne-*beme, streem, Jerusalem. Leeme* (= flame, A.S. leóma) is once only used exceptionally rhyming with *beme*.

97 *Two distinct classes of words in -eke.* So *cheeke, leke, seeke* (adj.), *seke* (vb.), *biseke, eeke, weeke* (s.), *meke*, and *unmeeke*, form one class yielding a large number of rhymes; *speke, broke, wreke*, form a second. Only once in all Chaucer have I found *eke* rhyming with *speke*, and once with *broke*. A third exception must be admitted in the rhyme of *speke* with *i-reke* = smoking, from A.S. réc. It is no doubt with *speke*, &c.,

---

* I have noticed also one exception (and there may be more) in the Cant. Ta. In the Prologue, l. 133, we have *eke* rhyming with *seeke*.

that Chaucer's *keke* and *queke* (Assembly of Foules) would have rhymed, had he used them at the end of lines; for the natural sounds imitated—those of the goose and duck—are much nearer to the French *é* (EE) than to (ii).

98. *Two distinct classes of words in -ede, with one or two exceptions.* When we turn to words in *-ede*, we seem at first to be in inextricable confusion. But three of these have two forms in A.S.; hence the difficulty. They are déed (=deed), dréd, bréd (=breadth), or less commonly déd, dréd, bréd. Setting these aside, and the anomalous prefix *-hede*, I find the other words clearly divisible into an (ii) and an (ee) class. The numbers of the rhymes they yield, with the exceptions, in those parts of Chaucer that I have examined, are as follow. The (ii) class: *nede*, 45−2; *bede* and *forbede*, 9−0; *spede*, 22−2; *hede* (=care), 25−4; *fede*, 9−2; *yede*, 5−0; *mede* (=reward), 8−0; *wede* (=herba), 1−0; *procede* and *succede*, 8−0; *blede*, 10−1; *glede*, 7−0; *erede*—again a classical word anglicized—2−0; *stede* (=horse), 1−0; *brede* (vb.), 1−0. It will be observed that (except the subst. *bead* derived from or identical with *bede*) not one of these words has been or is spelt with *ea* in its later form; while most of those which follow—all except *sede* and *wede*—are so spelt: vid. sup. § 84. The (ee) class: *dede* (=dead), 60−0; *hede* (=head), 66−1; *sede*, 8−2; *rede* (=red), 59−2; *rede* (=read, advise, advice), 72−1; *lede* (vb.), 29−4; *lede* (s.), 2−0; *mede* (=meadow), 16−0; *threde*, 4−0; *brede* (=bread), 6−0; *wede* (=vestis), 8−0. The affix *-hede*, and *dede* (s.), *drede*, *brede* (=breadth), rhyme chiefly with (ee) words, thus: *-hede* 46−8; *dede*, 66−19; *drede*, 84−31; *brede*, 12−5.

99. *Two distinct classes of words in -ete.* Words in *ete* can be classified in like manner: —with (ii) apparently, *swete* (adj.), *feet*, *flete* (vb.), *shete* (vb.), *shete* (s.), *mete* (vb.), *mete* (adj.) and *unmete*, *grete* (vb.), *quyete*, *bihete*, *planete*, *pete*; with (ee), *swete* (s.), *hete*, *wete*, *grete* (adj.), *whete*, *trete* and *entrete*, *plete* (=plead), *mete* (s.), *counterfete*. But some other terminations do not occur often enough for the distinction to be so satisfactorily made out that an argument can be built upon it. In all these cases however of which details have just above been given, we find two distinct classes of words. Distinct most assuredly; for the supposition that the symbol *e* always represents in Chaucer either the sound of (ee) or *any one* sound, is *utterly irreconcilable* with the facts above stated.

Mr. Ellis indeed recognizes (p. 751 note) the fact that Salesbury, to whom we are indebted for the earliest existing treatise (1567) on English pronunciation, claims 'diuersitie of pronounciation' for *e* in certain words, such as '*bere*,' beer or bear, '*pere*,' peer or pear, '*hele*,' heel or heal, and '*mele*,' ground corn or portion; and yet *without either authority or argument*, Mr. Ellis affirms that *e* was always (e) in Chaucer!

Just so Salesbury distinctly admits two sounds of *o*: Mr. Ellis allows Chaucer only one.

100 That the words of the former class in each case were sounded with (ii), is proved first and chiefly by the evidence of our dialects; secondly, by the existence of the (i) in many cases in the French form of the word; and thirdly, by some considerable amount of evidence which Holland and Germany afford, as shown in §§ 82 and 83.

In the former of all these pairs of classes the sound w s iii.

101 But what about the (e) class? That they were sounded with (ee) or (eei) I do not for a moment believe, except some words in -*ese*. One class of these contains the words *ese* (Fr. aise), with *disese, unese, misese; plese* (Fr. plaisier), with *displese; cease* seize (Fr. saisir); *appeise* (from O.Fr. pais peace); *preise* (O.Fr. proisier); and *reise* and *arreyse* (from O.N. reisa). All of these were probably sounded with (eei), keeping the (i) which we see in the O.Fr. and O.N. originals. But for the most part *bear, clean, release, dream, head, deal*, &c. utterly refuse to rhyme with *dispeyr, constreyn, harneys, claim, affraid, veile*, &c.* Just so in parts

In the second class of each of these pairs, the vowel was not (ee) r (eei) ex ceptions.

---

* Mr. Payne has quoted a few such rhymes (p. 593), but not from Chaucer, and in any case they are quite exceptional. But two centuries after Chaucer, the distinction, whatever it was, was quite obliterated. Hart and Bullokar give *great, near*, &c. with the same symbol for the vowel as *maintain, plain, reise*.

of Devonshire the pronoun *their* (dheeəɹ) is very differently pronounced from the adverb *there* (dheeɹ). The *e* and the *ai* or *ei* are symbols of sounds perhaps not far apart, but too far to rhyme. But the latter we seem to have fixed (§§ 58–67). What of the former? I have worked at the problem as follows.

102 *Can the sound have been (ææ)?* Tradition points to sóme (e) sound in these words, but it no more rhymes with (ee) on the one side than with (a) on the other. What intermediate sounds are there? Now we have many words in modern English, such as *apple, at, ash, axe, back, band, black,* &c. which have a common short vowel now—a genuine English sound, and one to which Mr. Ellis has repeatedly called attention,—and had a common vowel as written in A.S. also, viz. æ. And there is no evidence that I can find that these words have changed their sound for the last 1000 years. It seems probable therefore that in English they have always had the same sound, and this in the earliest stage of our language was represented by æ. Now why may not this same symbol (but perhaps with the accent) sometimes have represented a sound of the same quality but of greater length, so that the Somers. pronunciation of *Bath* (Bæːeth) shall be the true ancient sound of the word, and of the A.S. common noun bæð? This is at any rate a plausible conclusion, and helps us to understand why *heal* (hæːel), *deal* (dæːel), will not rhyme with *heel* and *feel* on the one hand, nor with *hail* and *sail* on the other.

103 *Objections to this view.* But two serious difficulties occur. First, if we have once now and then in Chaucer a long vowel rhyming with a short one, the latter is likely to be as nearly as possible of the same quality as the long one; as when *eke* and *lick* rhyme, or *bileve* and *give*. But when any of these (ee) words rhyme with others with a short vowel, not in a single instance do they rhyme with short (æ), but always with (e), as *heat* with *forget, dele* with *mantelle, temporel, eternel, pees* with *doutelees*. And in later times—for the same restriction on the rhymes continues with little or no relaxation, not only to Ben Jonson's time (as I have

§ 105]　　　　　'E' WORDS.　　　　　75

already shown), but at least as late as Dryden*—while *priest* rhymes with *Calvinist*, *beast* rhymes with *possess'd*, *meal* with *well*, *bread* with *fed*. The second difficulty is this: when these long vowels are shortened in course of time, they shrink not into (hæd), (læd), (dæd), (dæth), (bræth), (swæt), (thræd), &c., but (hed), (deth), (swet), &c.

104 *True sound that of (ee).* We seem therefore forced to the conclusion that these words in Early English had (ee) not (ææ). It is the sound of *a* in *mare*, or of the French *é*, and is incapable of forming a good and true rhyme either with (ii) or with (ee). You may search long in French poetry—*experto crede*—before you will find *chêne* rhyming with *peine*, or *fête* with *faite*, or *forêt* with *été*.

105 *This view confirmed by modern pronunciation.* And the pronunciation of many words even to the present day confirms this conclusion. Not only does the provincial (dhæa) or (dhееɹ) make a very bad rhyme with (dheer), (weer), (wheer), &c.; but before other letters as well as *r* (ee) and (ee) as rhymes are simply intolerable. Let *dead*, for instance, or *bread*, with the vowel a little prolonged—and it is long in these words in the Ormulum—be used to rhyme with *braid* (breed) or *played* (pleed); or *death* (deeth) with *faith* (feeth); and we feel at once that such a quasi-rhyme is insufferable. But this (ee) seems to be a less frequent sound in English than formerly, being supplanted in many words by (ii), as in (giiɹ), (spiiɹ), (iiɹ) *ear* s. (siid), (riid) v., (kliin), (biin) = *bean*, (spiik), (striim), (hiit), (whiit); in others by (ee), as in (greet), (breek); while in others in which a dental follows it is shortened into (e), as in (swet) = *sweat*, (hed), (led) *lead*, s.,

---

* It has never, I believe, been remarked that in Milton's rhymes and Dryden's, except that *a* has become (α), almost every distich would meet with Chaucer's approval, and the words that would not rhyme in Chaucer very rarely rhyme in Milton or even Dryden. Thus *fair* and *ear* rhyme with *tear* and *swear*; *meal* with *spread*; *sweat*, *eat*, *heat* with *great*; *far* with *repent*; *speak* and *weak* with *break*; and in all these cases the orthography, *ea* and never *ee*, fixes the sound as most probably (ee) not (ii); only rarely do we find such rhymes as *few* with *distress*, *lion* with *Absalom*, *ear* with *clear* or *appear*, *there* with *chere*. Yet these *ee* words do not rhyme with *ai*, or *a* words, as *speak* with *make*, except very rarely.

&c. But the abbreviating process is incomplete in some words; for no one sounds *dead, bread, thread, quite* as short as *led* and *bred*, or *breath* and *death* as low-*eth* and *Seth*, *breast* as *test*, and so on: to my ear at least the *ea* is still *a little* longer than the simple *e* in these words.*

106 *The distinction between the two classes of e words equally marked in Anglo-Saxon.* But as to the A.S. forms—and here we must deal largely with the symbols—more remains to be said. Especially I may observe that the (i) and the (e) classes, which Mr. Ellis, so fatally for his whole theory, confounds, are not less distinct in A.S. than they are in Chaucer. Indeed these classes, instead of converging as antiquity increases, diverge. The (i) and the (e) words, which are all written with one vowel in Chaucer, have five vowels or more in A.S. Thus: taking the 100 words which seem to be most clearly marked as (i) or as (e) words in Chaucer, I find 29 of the former are in A.S. written with *é*,† and 27 with *eó*;‡ and of the latter 12 are written with *e*,§ 19 with *ǽ*,∥ and 13 with *eá*.¶ It seems then that not only were the A.S. *é* and *eó* pronounced so similarly that they were easily merged in Chaucer's language in the one sound of (ii)—a fact which I have already (§ 79) endeavoured to account for; but the sounds of *e* in certain words, and *ǽ* and *eá* were also very close akin, as is proved by their having merged in the one (ee).

107 *The exact value of the Anglo-Saxon eá.* But what more exactly were the *eó* and the *eá*? They were not very remote from each other, for they were often interchanged, which I account

---

* See § 74 and foot note.

† Blédan, brédan, célan, cén, cépan, ewéman, ewén, déman, ée, fédan, geféra, fét, gléd, grén, grétan, hédan, hér adv., lée, méd, métan, sécan, séman, scén, spédan, stéda, swét, téð, wénan, wépan.

‡ Beó, beódan, beón, cneów, ereópan, deóp, deór s., deór a., fleón, fleótan, freó, gleó, leóf, neód, sceótan, seó, seóc, seón, seóðan, steóran, streón, teónan, treów, þeóf, þeón, þreó, weód (herba).

§ Bera, beran, derian, erian, -ere, spere, swerian, teran, werian: brecan, sprecan, wrecan.

∥ Ær, clén, dǽl, fǽr (timor), hǽlan, hǽr, hǽtu, hlǽn, hwǽte, Lǽdan, mǽd, mǽl, mǽnan, rǽdan, sǽd, þrǽd, wǽd, wǽron, wǽt.

¶ Beám, beán, breád, eáre, greát, leád, leáf, leás, -leás, reád, sceáf, steáp, teár.

for by the supposition that the accent in each of these diphthongs, though written on the second vowel, belonged equally or chiefly to the first. But the *a* in *eá* had greater tenacity of life than the thinner *ó* of the *eó*, as is shown by the fact that in so few words has it altogether disappeared, as it has in *eác* and *leác*, which in A.S. were also *ác* and *lác*, and these forms alone survived to Chaucer's time.

I take the true sound of these diphthongs to have been (iiu) and (iia).

That there was the (u) in the former of these, the accent belonging in fact to both vowels, is rendered probable by the numerous instances of *eó* words with by-forms in *y*, as *seón syn*, *treówe tryw̄e*, *fleós flys*; and by the instances in which the diphthong in inflexion changes into this vowel, as *freónd* and *feónd*, pl. *frynd* and *fynd*. For the sound of (y), which the A.S. *y* most probably represented, is in fact intermediate between (u) and (i), and it might therefore naturally result from their coalescence, just as (a) and (i) may coalesce into the intermediate (e), and (a) and (u) into the intermediate (o). And this (iiu) by Chaucer's time had become simple (ii) by the mere dropping of the feebler element in the dipthong.

108   *And of eá.*   *Eá* I believe to have been (iia), both on the ground of the spelling itself—for we may occasionally argue from orthography,—and because (i) and (a) are just the sounds that will naturally coalesce into the intermediate sound of (e), the very change which seems to have taken place in or before Chaucer's time. And if the manner of the change needs further explanation, there are certain A.S. forms which seem still to survive in the West of England, which throw the clearest possible light on this subject. Such are — assuming for the present what I shall presently endeavour to prove, that A.S. *á* (ee)— *greát* and *geá't*, *geáif* (or geaf) and *geá'f*, which still exist in Devonshire. (Giiat) or (giiat), and (giiav) or (giiav), very easily pass into (geeat) and (geeav), and then the (a) disappears. Whether the *ea* in A.S. was written with the

accent or not, would probably depend on the degree of emphasis which the writer attributed to the (i) sound. Perhaps (g*i*at) and (g*i*av) best represent the prevailing sound among old villagers in South Devon, in whose mouths however these words never reach the final stage of (g*ee*t) and (g*ee*v); but (giiat), (gi*i*at), (g*i*at), (geeat), (geet), all exist in Devonshire side by side and often used indifferently.

It has been already remarked that in some few instances, as *eác* and *leáe, eá* (like *eó*) simply loses its feebler element. Sometimes there are three forms even in A.S., as *seeáð, seéð, seá'ð* = sheath.

109   Having now dealt with what seem to be (ii) words, let
<small>Final argument us return to those written with *i*, about which
as to 'I' words.</small> there is this further fact to be noted: *desire, ire, sire, martire, wire, myre, hire, fire*, never rhyme with *here* and *manere** any more than these do with *there* and *where; shine, mine, fine*, &c., never rhyme with *quene, knene, kene*,† any more than these do with *elene* and *bene* (s.); *glide, wide, slide*, &c., never rhyme with *nede* and *spede*, any more than these do with *dede* (adj.) and *threde; nice, vice, justice, thries*, never rhyme with *gees* and *fleece;* and so on. Therefore, if we have reason to believe that these *e* words were sounded with (ii), we have here a further and final argument against the supposition that the *i* words which refuse to rhyme with them were so sounded.

When I find such sets of words as *ride, nede, brede; wine, queen, bean; fire, here, there; rise, bees, please; smite, swete, whete; time, seme, beme;* &c., in all of which the first obstinately refuses to rhyme with either the second or the third, which also will not in Chaucer rhyme with each other; nothing can be clearer than that in those we have three distinct vowel sounds, and *I must profess myself utterly unable to discern any vowels that have so good a claim to occupy the disputed places as those to which tradition*

---

* I have found one exception: *fere* (for *fire*) rhymes with *dere* and *here* (adv.) in Tr. and Cr., lib. iii.

† *Nine* I have found once rhyming with *grene*, and *engine* with *bene* (inf.).

points. Accept the voice of tradition; suppose the sounds to have been (ǝi) (ii) (ee) respectively, and all difficulty vanishes.

110 And now to return to the question started in § 9: was
Supposed tendency to change (ii) into (ǝi). there—or is there—a *tendency* in the Teutonic languages to change (ii) into (ǝi)? Many scholars suppose that in High German, Dutch, and English, the (ǝi) is simply a modern substitute for a more ancient (ii). The mode of writing in Early German, Low and High, favours this view; for the symbol was commonly *i*, and throughout modern Europe, England alone excepted, this stands for (i); and it is supposed always to have done so. Now let us see what this theory involves.

First, it involves the assumption that in far remote antiquity there was some one mother tongue from which alike the Teutonic and the Classic languages—we need not climb still higher up the family tree—were derived; and so long as it existed all words that we now sound with (ǝi) —*wine*, for instance—had (ii). It is sufficient to say that this assumption, however plausible, rests on no foundation of history or tradition. The one ray of light which the Mosaic records shed upon it (Gen. xi. 7) *seems* to make it doubtful. But this is treading on very slippery ground.

Secondly, it assumes that both Celts and Scandinavians in the north and the Latin and Hellenic races in the south persistently adhered to the (ii), and their (wiin) or (viin) remained and remains immutable.

Thirdly, that during long centuries and whole millennia the Teutons too—*tendency* notwithstanding—persevered with (wiin), until they learnt to write, adopting the Roman alphabet.

Fourthly, that the Latin *i* was always (ii), which is not certain, and can only be maintained by precisely such arguments as would prove the English *i* to have been always the symbol of (ǝi).

Fifthly, that after the Teutonic tribes had received the Roman alphabet—*post hoc*, not *propter hoc*—some of them, owing to this most curious tendency, came, at some period during the early middle ages, to change (ii) into (əi) : (wiin) no longer, but (wəin). Yet only some of the Teutons made this change: most of the Hollanders, the Frisians, and the peasantry who speak the Platt-Deutsch, retain (ii).

And all this is to be assumed in spite of the fact that there has been no such manifestation of the tendency in question since that period. After thousands of years during which it lay dormant, it came with a sudden and unaccountable gush, and has from that time sunk into torpor equally profound. For I hold it proved by the reasoning in the last few pages that there was a large class of (ii) words in Chaucer—not written with *i* but *e*—which have continued the same for at least the last hundred years.

Nor is there now any prevailing tendency, either in England, Holland, or Germany, to change (ii) into (əi). I do not mean that you may not find in some outlying districts a habit, purely local, of mispronouncing certain sounds, and in particular of mispronouncing (ii) in a manner approaching (əi), for this I admit as fully established; but as to the general speech of the people all over England, our *we, she, deem, seem, queen*, betray not the slightest inclination to become (wəi), (shəi), (dəim), &c.; nor the German *Lied, tief, Thier*, or the Dutch *lied, diep, dier*, to become (ləid), &c. We all have Teutonic mouths, and can judge each for himself whether we can detect in ourselves any such tendency.

Mere intermittent and partial tendencies cannot but be regarded with suspicion: if there really existed any such bias in the Teutonic mouth, why should it be exhibited in North Holland and not in Brabant? why in politer Hoch-Deutsch, and not in the Platt-Deutsch of the peasantry of the same district?

111 Finding this theory so unsatisfactory, I should prefer to suppose that the first divergence of the (ii) and the (əi) *Another view suggested as to the use of i.* divisions of the Teutonic race as to this particular of speech is not to be assigned to mediæval times, but is lost in the mists of far antiquity, and that the Latin *i*, when it is adopted to write these

languages—though I would not affirm with Lipsius that its proper sound was (ɔi)—yet had, or to Teutonic ears seemed to have, in the northern part of the empire,* besides the pure sound of (ii), at least in certain words or in certain mouths, a more or less perfect diphthongal sound approaching† that of (ɔi), so that it was capable of being used by different tribes as the symbol of different sounds.

In Ulphilas's Moeso-Gothic version of the gospels, we find most commonly *ei* substituted for *i* in proper names, as in Teibairius,‡ Seimon, Daweid, Peilatus, Paiaufeilu, Aileisabaiþ, Jaeirus, Beþsaeida, Galeilaia, and in many other borrowed words, as Helei Helei, Taleiþa Kumei, rabbei, rabbannei, &c. At first sight one might be disposed to ascribe this simply to itacism; but while Ulphilas doubtless stood in close relation to the Greek churches and their civilization, he also knew and wrote in Latin, and his alphabet, like his nominatives in -*us*, the *h* in such forms as *Abraham, Johannes, Beþlahaim*, is derived as much from the Latin as the Greek (witness his Latin F, S, and H, and disuse of the Greek Θ); and it seems probable therefore that he decided to use the *i* only for the pure sound of (i) or (ii) which was common to Greek and Latin, as in Christus, Filippus, Gabriel, Didimus, employing *ei* for the long diphthongal sound.

We thus seem to find an (ɔi), or a sound closely resem-

* As also in Lombardy; for I think we are forced to this conclusion by the remarkable statement of Sir Thomas Smith quoted in the foot note on p. 18 *supra*.

† It is obvious to remark that probably no two languages have precisely the same systems of spoken vowels. French and English for instance have scarcely—or shall I say, not—a single vowel-sound in common. Not to mention the French *u, eu, œ, &c.*, in French the vowel-sounds of our *it, sight, not, note, nut, wait, new*, are unknown; while our (ii) of *mean* is a fuller, and not merely a longer sound than that in the French *mine*, nor unless my ear deceives me, is the French *a* absolutely identical with our *a* in father, their *nette* with our *debt*, their *di* or *ai*, or *dis* with our *day*, their *poul* with our *pool*, and so on. And it is precisely these minute differences that constitute the almost ineffaceable distinction between the English of a native Englishman and that of a Frenchman who has lived even thirty years in England, and *vice versa*. (See also foot note on p. 7.)

‡ The *ai* stands to (eep or (e) beyond all reasonable doubt: see § 113; and the *iu* for (oo, see § 112.

bling it, in the earliest written German that is extant; while the same or a similar sound was written *i* or *í* in England, and probably in at least *one* word in Mœso-Gothic, *bi*, Germ. *bei*, Du. *bij.*, A.S. *bíg*.

This (əi), as being in the spoken language of those portions of the German race alike in Germany and in Holland which were endowed with the greatest intellectual or destined to achieve the highest political power, has become dominant and extended its rule with the spread of education, while the (ii), which survives in Platt-Deutsch and Flemish, has been abandoned to the inferior classes, amongst whom education and the far-reaching influence of fashion are fast stamping it out.

The Mœso-Gothic mode of writing the diphthong was not generally adopted till about the fifteenth century, the reason being simply that the rest of the Teutonic nations received both their religion and their mode of writing not from the East but from the West, not from Greek but Latin sources; and while diphthongs abound in Greek, they are but little used in Latin. While therefore nothing could be more natural than for Ulphilas, or the yet earlier missionary who first wrote Gothic, to use the diphthongs at his disposal to express in letters partly derived from the Greek the sounds of his native tongue, nothing was less to be expected than that those in the West who under similar circumstances employed an alphabet entirely derived from the Latin should make a similar use of it. It scarcely occurs to us now-a-days that it was a real stroke of genius, a great philological feat, to invent a diphthong, especially when the compound sound is somewhat difficult to analyse.

But Ulphilas's *ei* having at last come into more general use, this change of spelling has been commonly assumed to be an unfailing indication of a change of sound. A fallacious argument, as I believe; but even that cannot be alleged in the case of Anglo-Saxon and Early English. The change of pronunciation in German and Dutch being supposed to be sufficiently proved by the change of spelling, a like change of pronunciation is then assumed to have taken place in English also, where there has been no change of spelling. I think the evidence quite unsatisfactory in each case.

112 *Last words about (əu).* And how were the bishops and missionaries who first taught the Goths, the Allemans, or our Saxon sires the art of writing, to deal with (əu), supposing that sound to have been in use, as I believe it was, side by side with (uu)? Here not even Ulphilas had materials ready to his hand. Nay, I shall be told, he had *au*, which the modern Germans actually employ. True, Ulphilas had *au*, but it had a different sound to him. He found in it a fitting representative of the Greek ο. He had no symbol for (əu). Our Anglo-Saxon forefathers, when their turn came two centuries later, were in the same predicament. Both did the best they could with the appliances within their reach: they used the symbol that came nearest as they thought, namely, *u;* the Anglo-Saxons simply adding (not perhaps at first,* but in course of time) a diacritic mark, *ú*. It is not reasonable to expect them to have done otherwise. Moreover, neither Ulphilas nor Augustine would have been likely to find among his colleagues men who would readily adopt a symbol to which they were unaccustomed. Even now any *chanje* in our mode of spelling is not easily *introduc't, however accomplisht* and persuasive the writers who employ it; and probably Mr. Fry *iz* not very *sanguin az* to *hiz* chances of success with *dhe, dhat, enuff, gauz,* &c.; still less likely is it that scholars will be able to bring about the general adoption of any new letter or digraph, or even to restore a letter that was once in familiar use, as þ. However evident to philologists the advantages may be, they are not evident but to the few, and our conservative instincts rise in fierce rebellion against such *changes*. Just so in those early times, any novelty in spelling or in the use of alphabetic signs would be very

* I may have been in error in asserting (§ 45 supra) that the accents in A. S. "appear even in the earliest MSS. we possess," for in the Cotton MS., from which Mr. Sweet is publishing his admirable edition of Gregory's Pastoral Epistles, there appear to be no accents. Happily the error, if it is one, does not affect the argument of the passage.

slowly adopted, and it should excite no surprise if even centuries elapsed before *ou, au, uy*, etc., were invented and accepted, there being a general acquiescence in a simpler though more imperfect representation of the sound.

And now to return to AI words.

113 It is a theory that very obviously suggests itself, though not therefore necessarily a sound one, that any vowel-digraph must originally stand for the sound compounded of the two simple sounds represented. But be this theory true or false, it is not applicable in the case of our derived alphabetic systems. Ulphilas adopted vowel-digraphs already in use, and his *ai* was simply the Greek αι transferred to the service of the Gothic tongue. And what sound did αι represent? Not (ai) but (ee) or (ee). In modern Greek αι and ε are pronounced alike, "a little longer than the first *e* in *veneration*: further, *a* in *mate*, without the vanishing sound, expresses it almost exactly:" says Sophocles; and the codices Alexandrinus and Sinaiticus, by such forms as φοβηθηται (for -τε), αναβενων (for -βαινων), ιεροσολυμειτε (for -ται), Μακιδονια, &c., which are of very frequent occurrence, demonstrate the approximate if not entire identity of the sounds belonging to these symbols even earlier than the age of Ulphilas. The Greek ε moreover was equivalent in quality—I say nothing of quantity—to the *e* in Latin, which universal tradition makes (e). We may therefore confidently conclude that the Gothic *ains, aiþs, braids*, are identical in sound as well as in sense with the Dutch *een, eed, breed*, and the Gothic *airþa, bairgan, bairgs, wairþaiþ*, with the German *Erde, bergen, Berg, werdet*, and so on.

In like manner it is highly improbable that *ei* in Mœso-Gothic was used for (ee) + (i). *Ai* was (ee) or (ee), and the nice distinction between the *a* of *mate* with or without the vanishing sound was not likely to be observed when this branch of philological study was in its very infancy; just as Mr. Bell (as above quoted) points out that "the diphthongal quality of the English *ā* will not at first be admitted by every reader" even when his attention is called to it.

[side note: Is ai properly the symbol of (a) + (i)?]

114 *Two classes of ei words in Old High German.* The case is different with the symbol *ei* as used in western Europe, whether in England or Holland, in France or in Iceland, or on the Rhine. This *ei* was derived from the Latin, in which tongue it was never equivalent to *i*,* and, being rare, it is all the more likely to have been employed for the compound sound which it would at once suggest to the eye. If so, we have a large number of words—*ein, stein, leiten, -heit,* &c., a totally different set from those given in § 13—which have certainly undergone a change: these were sounded with (eei), (ĕei), or some such sound, which is now (ɔi).

When therefore we find in Old High German writings of the eighth century *i* and *ei* side by side in classes of words which are now both sounded with (ɔi), I believe the former of these symbols to have stood for a diphthong which was nearly (ɔi), the latter for a diphthong which was nearly (eei), which is strongly confirmed by the fact that in Mœso-Gothic (which the Vocabulary of St. Gall of the 7th cent. seems to follow) words of the latter class as a rule have *ai*, which we have seen was certainly (ee) or (ĕe): the former was nearly (æae) + (i), the latter nearly (ee) + (i); and these sounds being so near one another accounts for their having in course of ages run into one another, just as I shall show further on that the marked distinction between two classes of *eie* words in English became wholly obliterated between the times of Chaucer and the Elizabethan poets.

But to admit that a change of this kind has taken place is a very different thing from believing, in spite of important facts which contradict the belief, that in the Teutonic tribes there is a universal tendency to change (ii) into (ɔi).

115 The short *e* in Chaucer) and the unaccented *e* in A.S. *The short e in Chaucer was (e)* I believe to have been short (e); not merely however on the ground of such very slender

---

* The proofs are, 1st, that *ει* in Greek words always became *e* or *i* in Latin; and 2nd, that the Latin *ei* became *ηι* in Greek, as in Ἡράκλειος, Κικέρων, Ἀκύλιος.

† It will be borne in mind that many words have a short vowel now which had not in Early English, and vice versa, as *seven* (suven), devil (divl), *iron* (iurn), *red* (reed), *i.e.* [...] I have already not said that such inquiries are to a large extent inquiries about and abbut words.

evidence as the rhymes of Chaucer yield, but because all our dialects preserve this sound in the majority of these words, and their congeners in other languages in so many instances tell the same tale. In *sprecan*, Germ. sprechen, Du. spreken, and *brecan*, Germ. brechen, Du. breken; as also in *teran, beran, werian*, Lat. tero, fero, gero, the quantity seems to have changed by Chaucer's time, if not even in the time of Orm. But of many other words— whether of the Gothic stock, as bed, best, better, deck, edge, elbow, elf, fell (pellis), fennel, helm, hen, kettle, melt, nest, net, nettle, self, set (sedeo, ἕζω), west; or of classical origin, as excel, metal, pest, process, and a multitude of others—the equivalents in German, Dutch, and it may be other modern languages, all give the same sound both as to quality and quantity. The tradition is uniform. Hence my conclusion.

116 And what was the A.S. *ǽ*? Mr. Ellis supposes it to be A.S. *æ* (æǽ)? simply (æ) as in *hath* (Hæth) * prolonged as in the Somersetshire pronunciation of *Bath* (Bæǽth). This view is supported by the fact that in so many words the *ǽ* answers to the Ger. and Du. *a* or *aa*;† so that we might conjecture that at least in *early* A.S. the *ǽ* approximated to (aa), but at some time prior to Chaucer such words thinned off the vowel to (ee), there not being however sufficient evidence to show when this happened.

117 Five objections: true sound ee). But there are several weighty reasons for rejecting this hypothesis.

First, the traditional pronunciation in the West of England of the words which contained this *ǽ* is either with (ee) or (ee). E.g.: (ail seen teetsh Joee tee reed), i.e., I'll soon teach you to read; (kleen dhee dheea steeaz), clean they there stairs; (ai sim v z Amoost deed; iz breeth z

---

* That is, with the same vowel sound as in *hat*; not with the fuller *a* of *path*, as pronounced in some parts of England.

† A.S. sǽd, Du. zaad; A.S. rǽdan, Du. raden, Ger. rathen; A.S. mǽd, Ger. Matte, O.D. maede; A.S. prǽd, Du. draad, Ger. Draht; A.S. wǽd, Du. gewaad; A.S. hǽr, Du. haar, Ger. Haar; A.S. pǽr, Du. daar, Ger. dafr), M.G. thar; A.S. hwǽr, Du. waar, Ger. war; M.G. hwar; A.S. wǽron, Du. and Ger. waren; &c.

ver*i* we*e*k), I seem (= δοκέω - think, as commonly in Devonshire) he's almost dead: his breath's very weak,—or (Amoovst), (deevd), (breevth).

Secondly, *æ* when shortened, as in *ready, steady, any*, from *stǽdig, hrǽd, ǽnig*, has become (e), not (æ).

Thirdly, we have found evidence from various independent sources that one symbol in A.S. represented (aa), another (ii), and so on; and we have none yet for (ee), which we cannot do without.

Fourthly, we have seen ample evidence that the Norm. and O. Fr. *ei* was (ee), like the Icel. *ei;* and *heil* is Wace's form, quoted by Mr. Ellis himself on p. 531, for the A.S. hǽl, which is also the Du. heel, Frs. heel, Pl. D. heel, and Icel. heil.

And fifthly, if some of these *ǽ* words have Du. and Germ. congeners with *aa* or *a*, as shown just above in a foot note, a much larger number have *ee* or *e*, or in Icel. *ei*. Take for example (ex pede Herculem) words beginning with *lǽ-*: all, excluding derivatives, that I can trace in other languages are the following: *lǽce*, a leech (which as a proper name is often written *Leach*, and commonly pronounced (leetsh) in the West of England), M.G. lekeis, O.H.G. lákei, Sw. lakare, Dan. læge, Frs. leek; *lǽdan*, to lead, Icel. leiða, Sw. leda, Dan. lede, Frs. leda, Flem. leeden; *lǽfan*, to leave, Icel. leifa, Frs. lefa; *lǽm* (akin to lám loam), Du. leem, Ger. Lehm; *lǽnan*, to lend, Du. leenen, Ger. lehnen, and compare Pl. D. leen, Icel. len; *lǽne*, lean, Pl. D. leen; *lǽran*, to learn = teach, Sw. lära, Dan. lære, Du. leeren, Ger. lehren; *lǽs*, a leese or pasture, Ger. Lese (acc. Bosw.); *lǽstan*, to last, Pl. D. lessten; *lǽtan*, to let, M.G. letan, also Pl. D. laten, Ger. lassen, Ker. lazzan, Icel. láta; but in this last word, which gives the sole exceptional (a) among the (ee)s, it is doubtful whether the vowel is not really the short *a*, and not *ǽ*: neither Bosworth nor Thorpe accents the vowel, though Grein gives it long. These words beginning with *lǽ-* are a mere sample of what we find throughout the language, and the evidence of the whole immensely preponderates in favour of *ǽ* (ee).

118. *This coincides with results already reached.* We have already seen that the A.S. *eá* easily becomes (ee); the A.S. short *e*, being (e), if lengthened, will be (ee); and now we have reason to believe that *é* stood for (ee). All this perfectly coincides with another conclusion already independently arrived at, that Chaucer's *e* in the second of his two classes of *e* words was (ee). For Chaucer's English words with *e* are derived —I think without exception—from A.S. words in *é*, *eá*, and *e*. Such are séd, rédan, prést, létan, wéd, hwér, pér, wéron, wét, hwét, hér, méd, lén, ménan, clén; beám, reád, heáp, dreám, breád, leáf, leád, deád; beran, bera, derian, werian, brecan, sprecan, wrecan, swerian, &c. All these have the same vowel *e* in Chaucer.

119. *AW or AU was (AA), as at present.* Tradition gives us the sound of (A) in a considerable number of words, most of which are spelt with *au* or *aw*. Mr. Ellis, fixing his eye as usual on the symbol, sees two written letters, and, as "the orthography shows the sound," infers that two vowels were pronounced. But surely there is no very gross improbability in the supposition that our Anglo-Saxon and Early English ancestors possessed the simple sound in those words in which we have it; and that the spoken language has varied but little, while the written language has varied much amidst the throes and convulsions of a yet unsettled orthography; and that when the written *au* first became common in English, the novelty was only in the mode of representing a sound which itself was as old as the language. And the almost uniform evidence of tradition points strongly to this conclusion. All our dialects have a simple sound in these words, either (A) or a vowel very near (A); and not one of them, I believe, has a diphthong.

But what of the grammarians to whom Mr. Ellis appeals? Well, the 16th and 17th century authorities quoted by Mr. Ellis to prove that *au* was a diphthong seem to me to prove precisely the reverse.

120. *Gil's authority not adverse.* Gil's statements (1621) about all the vowels are intelligible from beginning to end on the simple supposition that he pronounced his vowels just as we do now, except only that *ŭ* was not as a rule (ɔ) but (u), and that words now written with *ea* were perhaps still pronounced with (ee).* Many differences in individual words there were undoubtedly, as *none* was then (noon), *once* (oons), *true* (trɹuu), *malady* (maladɔi), and so on; but no other in any large class of words. Gil thus read is easy to understand: as interpreted by Mr. Ellis, his language is more mysterious than the Egyptian hieroglyphics; though he has not, it is true, formally distinguished the short (a) from (æ), nor the German (*aa*) from (ʌʌ); and he seems to have had a trick of appending (u) to the one (?) word *awe*. There is little difficulty in all his work except to one who imports it, coming with a fixed resolve to make English in its earlier stages something very different from what it is now. And as to *au*, he says expressly of *laun* and *paun*: "Ubi adverte *au* nihil differre ab â," that is, from the *a* of *tall*.†

---

* I do not feel sure of this, because about half a century later (1685) Cooper so clearly gives the sound of (ii) at least to one word—apparently a typical word of this class, namely, *wan*. And here observe how readily intelligible Cooper's statements are as to the (ii) sounds, if you simply give him the benefit of a nineteenth century interpretation. He says for instance that the sound of *i* in the French *privilège* and the German *wider* is that which you have in *female, wean, gravity, deceive*. And again he says: "*I* quiesch in *adieu, conceiv, deceiv, either, friend, neither*." Nothing can be clearer, unless you are determined to misunderstand.

† Here are a few lists which I have made of words in Gil's orthography, illustrative of his "vocales quinque, omnes plurisonae," with my interpretation added.

1. Typical word *talou*: bark, wrath, thank, bad, water, was (also waz), hath, arm, chanʒ (= change), ar, baʒ (= badge), blak, kap, mari, harkn, chans, ax, glas, anger, ðat, hand, az, man, harsh, marchant, Hall (= Henricula·s), hav, part, star, starv, faðer (also faðer), gader, wash, land: *a* = (aa), (ai, ɑɹe), or (e).

2. Typical word *tal* (i.e. tale): wast, sam, chast, shav, hatful, kompar, lazi, faðer (also faðer), mak, havn, plas, hâl (= drag), skal, mal, aker, lam, kam, lat, patiens, grasious, statli, outraʒ, ladi, stavz, bas, daz (= dazzle), amaz, fonndasion; *a* = (ee) or (eɹ).

3. Typical word *til* (i.e. tall): walk, wâl, fâl, âlðoh, tâlk, kâl, advʌns, mortâl, total, prodigal, strâu, (also strʌ), drâ, denjâl, bâl (n.), bâl (vb.), hâl (n.); *a* = (ʌʌ).

4. Typical word *net*: wel (n.), them, best, wet, lent, whet, cheri, thens, peni, pens, end, hed, welth, brest: *e* = (e).

121 Bullokar, Hart, Smith, Salesbury, and Palsgrave, on *au*. Bullokar (1580) confirms this, making *au* to represent the same sound as *a* in certain cases, as *aul, aum, aun.*

As to Hart (1569), we cannot know with sufficient certainty what sound "the Dutch" gave to their *au*, nor how accurate an observer he may have been of the sounds of foreign tongues.

As to Smith (1568), Mr. Ellis has utterly misunderstood his expression when he speaks of "tanta soni commutatio." Smith is alluding to the sound of αυ as αβ (before vowels or sonants) or αφ (before surds) as in modern Greek! That was the modern corruption (at least so supposed) against which Smith and Cheke fought so vigorously and successfully.* Mr. Ellis's conclusion "So that his *au* was certainly (au)" is in no degree warranted by Smith's language.

5. Typical word *nēt* (i.e. neat): dēth, lēvn, pērch, brēd, prēch, ēch, indēvor, bēst (= beast), lēf, zēl, ēgl, ēz, ēt, grēt (magnus), nēuer, brēk, plēze, ðēr, lērned, instēd: *ē* = (ee) or (ee͞), etymological reasons alone, I suspect, causing these words to be written with *e* rather than *ä*.

6. Typical word *win*: briʒ (= bridge), skil, kin, mil, thik, quins, thistl, children, liv, which, witnes, Ingland, king, wimen, with, kis, prins: *i* = (i).

7. Typical word *wīn* (i.e. ween): hī, ðī, mī, yī, tu sī, hwīl (sive huīl), chastitī, kīn, sīm, bī (vb.), shīld, pīpl, quīn, chīk, bīf, shīp: *ī* = (ii) or (*ii*).

8. Typical word *wjn* (i.e. wine): mjn, ljf, enemj, euerj, adulterj, wjf, fjn, swjn, twjs, tjm, chjld, wrjt, kjn, aerj, sjlent, bisjd, qujt, wjz, kaitjv, eksŭdinglj, ðjself, lj, opmlj: *j* = (ai).

9. Typical word *pol*: hors, klok, not, box, ornament, omnor, long, strong, sorro, born, flok, skorn, shok, soft, blok, ox, oxn, foli, rod: *o* = (o).

10. Typical word *pōl* (i.e. pole): yōk, brēd, abrōad, gōld, hōli, hōlsum, kōl, hōst, glōri, hōp, rōs (n.), hōm, ōn (unus), ōns (= once), hōz, ok, trōa (vb.), skōr: *ō* = (oo) or (*oo*).

11. Typical word *ūz* (i.e. use, vb.): pvr, trv, yvth, rvl, svr (certus), demvrlj, natvr, hvz, ʒvlins, virtv, endvr: *v* = (Juu).

12. Typical word *us*: wud, wul, wuman, wurd, bruðer, ʒuʒ (judex), put, wurði, gud, trubl, muni, hurt, dung, duzn, bush, luv, Lundon, tung, punish: *u* = (u).

13. Typical word *ūz* (i.e. ooze): mūn, nūn, tū (duo), spūn, mūsik, mūv, būk, shūld, dū, yū: *ū* = (uu).

14. Gil writes dispair rh. w. fair, which is elsewhere fāir, faier, and fāier; also aier (n), dai, strāi, retāin, restrāin, swāin, disdāin: *ăi* or *ai* = (ee͞).

* So Butler condemns the sound of *eu* as taken from the Byzantine pronunciation of *ευ*: "Therefore they err grossly that for Eunuke [i.e. eunuch] say Evnnke, for Eutykus, Evtykus." (In modern Greek β almost = the Engl. *v*.)

Salesbury again (1547) shows that *aw* had the sound of *a* in *balde, ball, wall.** Were these words really sounded (bauld), (baul), (waul), as Mr. Ellis tells us? It is hard to reconcile such a supposition with the teachings of etymology. *Wall* is the A.S. *weall* or *wall*, O. Du. and Flem. *walle*, Ger. *Wall*, Lat. *vallum*, Dev. (waal), Northumb. (wææl), and so on: where is there a trace in any of these of an almost distinct syllable (u) which thrust itself in for a time only to be ejected with ignominy after a brief usurpation?

Lastly, Palsgrave (1530), the earliest authority to whom we can appeal, uses *au* to express the *a* of the French *chambre, taut, quant,* &c. Are we then seriously to be told that the French descendants of the Latin *camera, tantus, quantus,* &c. at one time admitted an almost distinct syllable (u) after the (a), and that it has again disappeared? It is certain that the *a* in those French words approaches our *au* (A), and even now there are books which teach English learners so to sound it.

The case of French words of Latin derivation in which *al* was followed by another consonant differs widely from that of *chambre*, &c. Such words are the modern representatives of *aliquis, altus, altare, alter, calcarium, calefacere, calx, falco, falx, saltare.* Here we have abundant evidence of an intruder—a usurper rather. The *l* first assumes an ill-defined introductory sound or glide, as in the Dev. (skɐɐɔl) for (skuul) above remarked on, § 79; then this glide developes into a full (u) or (o), as in *aulcun, aultre, aultel;* next the (o) drives out the *l*, as is shown in the Meigret's *aotre, loyaos, faote;* and finally this (o) absorbs the (a), as in the modern pronunciation of *autre*, Sp. *otro*, Port. *outro*, &c. There is no evidence of a similar insertion before *m* or *n*. Only when the *m* or *n* is final, and is then (through Celtic influence, as I have elsewhere remarked)

---

* According to the grammarians *a* used to be pronounced as *au* before *lk, lf, lm, n,* and *nt*. As to *aunge*, Gil gives *aunge* (unless his *aung* is simply a misprint for *ahng*) with the same vowel as *arm, l's, az,* &c.; Butler pronounces the *a* as *au* in this word, as we do now, adding that it is still called *chaunge* in the North in common with *straunge, aun d, daunger,* &c.

122 A.S. æ = (æ), e
short = (e), and i
short = (i).
I have overlooked, or somehow failed to find, any statement of Mr. Ellis's *reasons* for holding that the A.S. unaccented *æ*, *e*, and *i* or, in *late* A.S., *y*, were (æ), (e), and (i). To his conclusions however I assent, and for this reason, that in the great majority of words that were written with these vowels, an almost unvarying tradition gives those sounds. For example, *ælmesse*, *appel*, *æsc*, *æsce*, *æt* (prep.), *æx*, *bæc*, *bænd*, *cæppe*, *clæmian*, &c., are all pronounced, as has been already pointed out in regard to some of them, in modern English (æ); though *æg* has changed *æ* into (e); *æfter*, *bæð*, *blæst*, *cræft*, into (aa); and *blæd* into (ee)—unless indeed the true form was *blǽd*, or, as seems not unlikely, the two *blæd* and *blǽd* existed side by side, and the latter alone has survived. So bedd, belcettan, bell, belt, bene, bendan, beria, betera, betst, bletsian, cempa, Cent, cetel, cwellan, &c. are sounded with (e); and many of the continental kinsmen of these words have the same sound, as Icel. bed, Dan. bed, Du. bed, Ger. Bett, and so on. And again, bicce, biddan, bil, bin, bisceop, bitter, blis, bringan, cicen, cinn, clif, clingan, clyppan, cnyttan, crib, cwic, cyn, cyning, cyssan, &c., are sounded with (i); though *cild** has become (tshsəild), and *climan* is now

---

* Or should it not be *cīld*? The vowel is long in the singular in the Ormulum, and short in the plural, just as at present.

Since this sentence, and indeed the whole essay, was written, Mr. Furnivall has called my attention to an interesting and carefully-written paper on this subject in the Transactions of the American Philological Association, 1871. It is "On English Vowel Quantity in the Thirteenth Century and in the Nineteenth," by the late Mr. James Hadley (obiit 1872), Professor of Greek in Yale College. No careful reader of the Ormulum will be surprised to find that Mr. Hadley's conclusion is "that in the great majority of cases the vowels which had a long sound six hundred years ago are long now, those which had a short sound then are short now." My contention is that, as a general rule, our vowels have remained unchanged in quantity and quality alike. Combine Mr. Ellis's view with the result of Professor Hadley's investigations, and you are forced to believe—as to the long vowels—that a whole series of forcibly pronounced sounds has undergone a simultaneous change into another widely different series of sounds equally forcibly pronounced.

§ 125]   SHORT 'A.'   93

(klɔim), but in provincial English (klim) still. Here again our conclusion is fortified by Icel. bitur, Da. bitter, Sw. bitter, Du. bitter, Pl. D. bitter, Ger. bitter, &c. &c.

123 *A.S. a short æ (a).* Short *a* in Anglo-Saxon was also probably (a),* though that sound has now almost died out except before *r* and in provincial English. It may however often be heard in Devonshire, as in (kandl), (man), &c., where the politer pronunciation gives (æ).

124 *The sounds of æ and e very near each other: the modern pronunciation of ate.* That æ was not very remote from *e* is shown by the numerous by-forms such as *fæst fest, æfter efter, hæn hen, stæppan steppan*. Instances are not numerous in which only a form in æ having existed (so far as is known) in A.S., this æ has become (e) in modern English. Such however are *æg = egg, læss* less (on which see below) and *æt* ate, when this is pronounced, as commonly, (et); but when pronounced (eet), this is properly the plural from *æton* : (et) and (eet) really differ just as *sang* and *sung*.

125 *Chaucer's short e: less, lasse; lefte, lafte.* And as to the short *e* of Chaucer. Mr. Ellis, reasoning as elsewhere from the exception rather than the rule, finds the double forms *lesse lasse, lefte lafte*, and thinks (p. 263) these "indicate that *e* short was occasionally pronounced as broadly as (a)." He adds, "Perhaps the *e* was generally broad, as (E) rather than (e)." Strange that he does not perceive that while almost every word with the short *e* in Chaucer (bed, reck, -ness, leg, &c.) had the short *e* in the earlier A.S. or O.N. form (bed, recc, -nes, leggr, &c.), and has it still, these two words had *not* the same vowel in A.S., but æ—*læssa, læfde*. In Chaucer's time the transition from (ææ) or (æ) to (e) was yet incomplete. *Læssa* and *læfde* have now in fact undergone precisely the same change as *æt* into (et), and *wæt* into (wet);

One would surely imagine that energy of tone would tend to produce permanence of character in the sound.

* Or (a'; b'). I will not follow Mr. Ellis in the chimerical attempt, on mere conjecture, to mark such minute distinctions in the speech of men who lived a thousand years ago. Doubtless words then as now were slightly different in different mouths, even when the sound was supposed to be the same.

but in Chaucer's time the old form and the new apparently coexisted, just as the English *die* coexisted with the O.N. *dey*, and *parde* with *pardy*. But they furnish not the shadow of an argument for a broad sound of the *e* in words which had not the *ǽ* or *œ* in A.S.

126 The final *e* when sounded.   As to the unaccented final *e* in Chaucer, I may venture to repeat here what I have said in the Foreword to my edition of Grosseteste's Castel off Loue, page v.: "My theory is that whenever the final *e* represents a final *syllable* in Anglo-Saxon [or Old Norse or French], it *may*—not *must*—be sounded. See notes on ll. 32, 331, and 830, and Glossary s. vv. *Drihte, Boþe, Wiþoute*." But the question remains whether the precise sound of this -*e* in Chaucer was that of the final *e* in French, or in German, or was like our -*y* in *many, happy*, &c., or what it was.

127 Final *e* not (ii), nor (i).   Assuming that the final accented *e* in Chaucer is proved to have been (ii),—for I hope some at least of my readers will have been so convinced—the first question that now suggests itself is whether the unaccented *e* might not have been the same, or at least a close approximation to it; so that we might take it to be the (i) which we now write as a final *y*. There is this difficulty: Chaucer's final *e* was often dropped, especially before an initial vowel in the next word, and (i) seems to be too sharp a sound to be easily so elided. But a weightier objection is this: that final *e* in a large number of cases stands for -*en*, and there is no reason to believe that this was ever (iin). On the contrary, the Ormulum makes it clear that the vowel in this termination, as also in -*es, -est, -etti, -ed, -er, -ness*, was short. Ormin's spelling is *ennglessh*, angels, *findesst*, findest, *findeþþ*, findeth, *fullhtredd*, baptized, *faderr*, father, *haliȝnesse*, holiness; and so also *findenn*, to find, *we lufenn*, we love, *biforenn*, before, *wiþþutenn*, without, and so on.

128 Final *e* was (v).   But let us pursue the line of thought which the first of these two objections to (i) suggests. Every one knows how strong a tendency there is to pronounce a final unaccented syllable indistinctly, and to substitute all the short vowels in such cases by (e), as when we hear for *to-morrow, window, thorough, gentlemen, anvil, beloved—tamorra, winda, thora, gemmun, anvul*, and (at least in the Western counties) *belovud;* and indeed in very many words this is either the accepted, or a very common, mode, as in *madam, my lord, cardinal, evil, devil,* bishop, chariot, pigeon, porpoise,* and all words ending in *-tion* or *-sion, -al, -an, -ar, -on*, and *-ous*, and many besides. In all of these the tendency to, or the full adoption of, (e) in the last syllable is obvious. And even (nearly) five centuries ago the same tendency showed itself, as when for instance in some of the oldest MSS. of Chaucer we find such spellings as *bysmoterud, pepul*, &c., which certainly, as thus written, were not pronounced with (e) in the last syllable. It is therefore evident that very shortly after, if not even during, the lifetime of Chaucer, this habit existed. Moreover we have a large class of words in which the final consonant has or had a written vowel preceding it, which is not pronounced; especially many words ending in *-en*, as *garden, oxen*, and in *-le* (formerly *-el* or *-ol*), as *temple, apostle:* in all of these the vowel seems to have sunk into the condition of a short (e) before it finally disappeared; indeed there is even now such a short vowel dimly audible in many of these words, as *temple*. And in Chaucer we find a large number of words just at that stage where the final *e* is vanishing; when it might be used, or might be omitted, according to the exigencies of the metre, or at the pleasure of the reader. The probability is therefore that at that time it had just that sound which could most readily be elided, namely (e). We then get this series of sounds for such a word as *above* from King Alfred's time to our own: (abuuvan), abuuv'en , (abuuv'e), (abuuv'e), (abuuv), (abɔv), the written form being *abufan, aboven,* and *above*.

129. *The short final e in A.S. was probably (e.)* As to A.S., the short final *e* in inflexions (ic lufige, to cySanne, hine selfne, &c.) not being liable to elision in that earlier stage of the language, we

---

* But in fact, as the older forms show, it (evl) and (devrl), like (aidlu) and (moidlu), are simply corrupt pronunciations, however to be noble.

could not expect a change into (v), and the sound was most probably (e): not (ii), for then we should be likely to find such forms as *ic lufigeó, to cyðanncó* (or with *-á*), and so on ; but none such, I believe, ever occur.

But would not this argument prove that the A.S. *he* and *me* were short, (he) and (me)? They may have been so.

130 *Me, he, thee, we, ye, in Anglo-Saxon with (e); in Early English with (v); in both also with (ii).* The forms *mec* and *mech* which occur in Cædmon may have had a short vowel like the Icelandic *mik*, M.G. *mik*, Da. and Swed. *mig*, and Ger. *mich ;* and the final guttural being lost, the short (e) would remain. And just as Mr. Ellis believes that many (e) words—these very words for example—have in course of time assumed an (ii), and as beyond doubt very many have done so, these words may have undergone such a change between the ages of Cædmon and Chaucer. It is in fact exactly the same change as all Greek words with η have undergone in the process of itacizing. And yet there is no reason why older forms may not still have survived in occasional use. And so I have no difficulty in understanding the exceptional rhyme in C. T. 673, 4, where it will be observed that there is no ictus on the *me*—

> That streight was comen fro the court of Rome (ruu·me)
> Ful* loude he soong come hider loue to me (luu·vɐ tuu·me).

Or (ruu·mv) (tuu·mv) : or this may have been an imperfect rhyme. The *me* here is the archaic apocopated form of *mee ;* but the common sound nevertheless, and the only one when the ictus rested upon it, was (mii), rhyming with *be* (A.S. beón), *three* (þreó), *thee* prosper (þeón), *tree* (treów), *free* (freó), &c.

And as *me* was apocopated, so were *he*, which has lost a final *s* or *r* as in the M.G. *is*, Lat. *is*, Ger. *er ; thee*, which is *þik* in Icel., *thuk* in Mœso-Gothic, *dich* in Ger.; *we*, which is *vèr* in Icel., *weis* in M.G., *wir* in Ger. ; and a final *r* or *s*

---

* Mr. Furnivall writes *ff:* erroneously, I venture to think. The Gothic capital *f* having a double downstroke looks like the double letter. Why should *ful* at the beginning of a line have two *f*s, and never otherwise?

appears at the end of the Icel., M.G., and Ger. equivalents for *ye*. All of these *may* therefore have been (he), (dhe), (we), (Je). Suppose it so, yet all of these had before Chaucer's time submitted to the change of vowel which Mr. Ellis supposes to have occurred some centuries later. Yet not to the utter exclusion of older forms. So Chaucer rhymes *sothe* with *to the*, that is (suu·the) (tuu·dhe) or (suu·thɇ) (tuu·dhɇ), or the rhyme may have been imperfect; and elsewhere *swithe* with *hy the;* but there is no ictus on the *the* in either of these; and the use of *'a* for *he*, as in the phrase *quoth 'a*, is familiar not only in the mouth of Mrs. Quickly, but in modern provincial English. So (dhɇ) for *thee*,* (mɇ) for *me*. And probably other such forms are in use. But while admitting that these pronouns *may* have been so sounded, the accented forms *mé* and *þé* which occur in Cædmon (if Thorpe's edition may be trusted) point to a different conclusion.† Perhaps a thousand years ago as at present both forms existed side by side.

131 Y probably represented (y). Many arguments—such for instance as that which I have used on *dyde*, §53,—based on derivations of words and forms might be adduced to show that *y* in early A.S. was akin to (u) and was probably (y), and *ý* was probably (yy); while in course of time the (yy) changed into (ii)—as also in both Icelandic and Greek— and finally even within the A.S. period, *i* and *y* came to be used indifferently. This was evidently the case, at least in part, even when those MSS. of Gregory's Pastoral Care

---

* *Th' Song of Solomon* (Cornw.) has. "When I shud find *tha* outside, I wud kiss *tha*;" and Mr. Baird gives us the following: "Stay *ma* way slaggins, komfut *ma* way happles." *The Song of Solomon*.

"Here Rabin Vinch whose haid ad zunk
Look up an zeth—Bit wad I'n *he* drunk?"
Nathan Hogg's Letters, p.

"Deei Jan, yu hant niver zeed zawjers to drill,
Zo I'll gie *thee* a huisite intoot if yu wull."
Ibid. p. 11.

† Cædmon has a also, whence ... *Zoser*; while (dh) was probably the original of the later *utsh* and the modern *Somer-o-hire oshe*.

were written which Mr. Sweet is now editing for the E.E.T. Society; for many words are there spelt with *y*, in both MSS., which have no affinities to words with a radical *o* or *u*.

132 Short O. To the short *o* both of A.S. and of Chaucer Mr. Ellis assigns the sound of (o); and as I see from the top of p. 226 that this (o) is the *o* of *cross* and *gone*,* I am happy to be able to assent to his conclusion. He seems to me also to have proved his point as to short *u* as being commonly the symbol of (u) or (*u*). But of this more anon.

133 The sound of the long *u* as (ju) is now commonly regarded as distinctively English, and this sound I believe, on the evidence of almost uniform tradition, to have been familiar in a small class of English words, though written otherwise than with the simple *u*; as in *treowe*,† *getrywe*, *bleó*, *niwe*, *new*, *heaw*, *iw*, *iwh*, *euwa*, *meu*, *Lœwes*, &c.

The quasi-diphthongal u, *so written, found only in French words.* But it is exclusively in words of French derivation that the simple *u*—the written symbol —now has this sound of (ju),‡ except only *pure*, *mule*, and *cucumber*; the first two of which being also French words may easily have adopted a French sound as more fashionable, and in some such way the exceptional *cucumber* may probably be accounted for. *Now* the French sound of *u* is (y); and French pronunciation is

---

* Distinguishing it from the *o* of *on* and *odd*, which he writes (ɔ). But in fact there is no such difference between *gone* and *on*, when the latter is used adverbially ("Pray go *on*"), though when *on* is a preposition, we do cut the sound a little shorter: that is all. Indeed sometimes *gone* is made quite as short as ever *on* is. In "He's gone *on*," is not the *gone* the shorter of the two? And as to *odd*, the vowel is still the same, except that it is necessarily sharpened by the *d*, as all vowels are when followed in a close syllable by an explosive mute.

† There is, I think, ample proof producible from various writers from Palsgrave to Cooper that many words which we now sound with the simple (uu), such as *true*, *blue*, *rude*, *rule*, *flute*, *drew*, *dew*, had formerly the quasi-diphthongal sound, as (trjuu), (bljuu), &c.

‡ Mr. Ellis writes (iu) or (iuu), yet he makes the pronoun *you* (juu). Is this an oversight? Or does he really think educated Englishmen pronounce *you* and *u*-nion at all differently?

unchanging, French tradition trustworthy; therefore *u* was (y) two, three, four, centuries ago; therefore also our (Ju) is a modern corruption: so Mr. Ellis seems to reason.

134. *The French u had formerly a diphthongal sound.* But with all deference I think we have abundant evidence that the French and Scots formerly sounded *u* as a diphthong, and that we have preserved the true sound. Baret, 1573—I quote from Mr. Ellis—speaks of the Scottish *u* as "rather a diphthong than a vowel, being compounded of our English *e* and *u*" (p. 168). Somewhat earlier, Hart, 1569, describing the Scottish sound of *gud* and the French *fust* (i.e. *fût*), says expressly, "you shal find the sound of the diphthong *iu*,* keping both the *i* and the *u* in their proper vertu" (p. 7,,6). He also implies (ibid.) that the pronoun *you* has the same sound, when he asks: "What difference find you betwixt the pronoun *you* and *u* in *gud* and *fust*?"† Smith, 1568, says the French *u* "per se" was sounded like the English *yew* (p. 166). Salesbury, 1547, writes some of these words with *uw*, which, as I have elsewhere observed (see § 5), every Welshman pronounces like, or as nearly as possible like, our *you* (Juu). Then again, for I admit that sometimes and to a certain extent "the orthography shows the sound," the prevailing orthography of many of these English words has been in every age with a digraph or other compound symbol, from *iw* in A.S. to *ew* now-a-days (see p. 98 supra), including Palsgrave's complicated *ewu*, and

---

* In his new orthography he writes *us* (noun), *use* (vb.), *abuse*, *you*, *rule*, as *ius*, *iuz*, *abiuz*, *iu*, *ruid*.

† An instructive passage from Hart's book is the following: "Now to come to the *u*. I sayde the French, Spanish, and Brutes, I maye adde the Scottish, doe abuse it with vs in sounde, and for consonant, except the Brutes as is sayd: the French doe neuer sound it right, but usurp *ou* for it, the Spanyard doth often vse it right as we doe, but often also abuse it with vs: the French and the Scottish in the sound of a diphthong: which keeping the vowels in their due sounds, commeth of *i*, and *u*, (or verie neare it) is made and put together vnder one breath, confounding the sounds of *i*, and *u*, togither." These words "or very near it" fully warrant the conclusion that the French and Scottish "abuse" was to make their quasi-diphthongal *u* (ïyy), while the English "abuse" was to sound *u* as (Iuu). This passage has, I believe, been overlooked by Mr. Ellis.

Bullokar's *eï*, *eÿ*, and *eẅ;* and even words of French derivation are often written with such combinations, as *vertuwes*, &c., in Chaucer.

135   *This quasi diphthong was composed of the same elements as our long u (juu).*   If we accept this mass of direct and positive evidence for a diphthongal sound as represented by the symbol *u* in French and in Scottish, and in many English words, the question arises, of what elements is this diphthong compounded? Salesbury, as I contend, gives a clear answer. And Hart distinctly affirms the antiquity and authority of "the Italian and high Dutch and Welshe pronounciation of their letters" in opposition to "our errors" (Pref. p. 5); as elsewhere he writes: "To perswade you the better that their auncient sounds are as I have sayde, I report me to all Musitians of what nations soeuer they be, for *a, e, i,* and *o:* and for *u* also, except the French, Scottish, and Brutes [i.e. Welsh] as is sayd." What can be clearer than that the *i* and *u*, which according to Hart make up the diphthong in question, are to be sounded as the Italians and Germans and all musicians sound them, viz. as (i) or (ii), and (u) or (uu)? Examples from Hart are t*ee*th and m*ee*t, instruments and the French *ou*. And surely these sounds when compounded yield the diphthong which we now hear in *use* and *abuse*. Yet, strange to say, Mr. Ellis cites Hart as a witness to the sound of *u* as the non-diphthongal (y)! But again, Hart, after describing the five vowels, adds: "And holding the top of your finger between your teeth, you shall the more sensiblye feele that they are so made with your say'd instrumentes." Can Mr. Ellis perform the feat of sounding (y) with his finger between his teeth? I have heard a member of our Society make the attempt, and he satisfied his own ears, but by no means mine. In fact (aa) (ee) (ii) (oo) and (iuu) can be easily sounded just as Hart suggests: (yy) cannot possibly be so sounded, and this test effectually excludes it from Hart's list of English vowels.

I find too that Mr. Ellis believes, as I do, *you* to have been pronounced even in Chaucer's time just as we now sound it—(Ju) or (Juu), (p. 719, ll. 720 and 728). But Hart writes it *iu*. Was there then an "interregnum" between Chaucer's time and ours in which this pronoun was sounded (yy)? The exigencies of a foregone conclusion have not often driven a man further in the direction of the utterly absurd, than when they impelled Mr. Ellis to say (p. 168): "Thus Hart writes: (wi did not mutsh abiuz dhem), meaning (wi did not mutsh abyyz dhem) as I shall hereafter transliterate his *iu*."

136 *Mr. Ellis's transliterations.* It is much to be regretted that Mr. Ellis has not perceived how immensely his transliterations detract from the value of his book. Where old writers on pronunciation, who have adopted a special orthography expressly to endeavour thereby to convey their meaning more clearly, are cited as authorities, but with Mr. Ellis's newly devised orthography substituted for their own, not only does this—so far as the argumentum ex auctoritate is concerned—utterly nullify the argument, which thus becomes a mere begging of the question, but it also deprives the reader of all chance of forming an independent judgment by means of the passages adduced.

137 *Objections to u = (yy) from Cheke and Smith.* But while I contend that the long *u* in words of French derivation was sounded as a diphthong, the startling objection occurs that the Greek *v* with which Cheke* identifies it "simplex est: nihil admixtum, nihil alienum, adjunctum habet;" "and it was therefore," Mr. Ellis adds, "a pure vowel, with which he identifies the English long *u*." The difficulty is not hard to clear up. The Scottish *u* has at least two sounds. In most parts of Scotland it is at present the French *eu* (eee) but approaching the *u* (yy). But in some parts it is sounded after the gutturals, as I am credibly informed, and as I believe I have myself heard it, with an interposed (j), just as the same semi-vowel is appended in Icelandic to *k* and *g* before the so-called "weak vowels." Now Cheke was writing about Greek pronunciation, not English, except incidentally, and

---

* There are very few misprints in Mr. Ellis's book, but on p. 165 for "Græcum v sonuemus," *leg.* "Græcum v sonamus," and before "adjunctum" *leg.* "alienum," as above.

the Greek υ being the simple (yy), his mind dwelt only on such words as (pœœr)* and (sœœn) or (pyyr) and (syyn) for *poor* and *soon*. Smith and Hart were writing about English pronunciation—Mr. Ellis's quotation from Smith on p. 166 is from the *De recta et emendata Linguæ Anglicæ Scriptione*—and hence they naturally thought of that Scottish sound which more resembled the particular English sound they were dealing with, viz. that which included the semi-vowel, as the English *yew* and the Scottish—not (gœœd) or (gyyd), but—(gjœœd) or (gjyyd). *Gud* is the one Scottish word which Hart quotes repeatedly (see Ellis p. 796): and we can easily understand how he may have considered the (jœœ) or (jyy) a diphthongal sound.

138 *The true sound of u in French and Scottish was (jyy).* Hart takes the French and Scottish sounds to have been quite equivalent, and in his time that may have been the case: indeed to many ears the Scottish and French *u* now may seem to have the same sound, and in some parts of Scotland there may be no difference. But whatever doubt there may exist as to the exact sound of the Scottish *u*, I do not suppose the French sound to have been (jœœ). At any rate the traditional pronunciation of *neuf, peut, peuple, jeune*, &c., combined with their varied spelling in early authors, leads me to the conclusion that the sound of (œ) was not represented in Early French by *u*, but by *ue, eu, oe*, and *eo*. Yet if *u* was not the sign for (œ) it *may* have been for (jœ); but accepting the evidence of tradition, I think it more likely on the whole to have stood in French for (jy) or (jyy).

That this French (jyy) and Scottish (jœœ) or (jyy) was not quite the English (juu), but "verie neare it" is admitted by Hart in the passage quoted in the footnote on p. 98. We pass on to EW.

139 *Two classes of EW words according to Palsgrave.* But as these sounds of (juu), (jœœ), (jyy), approached one another very closely, it does not seem improbable that three or four centuries ago custom may have sufficiently varied even among

---

* I do not of course mean the open sound of the French *jour*, but the thin vowel of *jeune*, approaching (yy).

"the better learned" for some to have used one of these sounds in certain words, and others another, for we know that there were differences of old as to many words, just as there are now. If therefore we think we have now satisfactory reason to believe that the French *u* in Palsgrave's time, 1530, was (Jyy), we can understand that he pronounced the words *rewe* (an herbe), *mew* (for a hawke), *clew* (of threde), and *trewe* with this (Jyy), but sounded *dewe, shrewe, fewe* with some different sound—see Ellis's quotations, pp. 137 and 163; while yet Smith knew no such difference. Did Palsgrave imagine a difference which did not exist? or did it exist in his day and soon afterwards die out altogether? There is undoubtedly a difficulty about the words which it was long the habit, as it still is partially, to spell with *ew*: will Chaucer help us to find our way out of the labyrinth? We may at least learn something of the usage of his day.

140 *There are in fact three such classes.* In this hope I have once more gone through the whole of Chaucer, including the poems attributed to him,* taking Bell's edition, and collected all the rhymes of words of this class. The following tabular statement will exhibit them all, 202 in number.

* It is between two and three years since I went through the first 12,481 lines; the rest I have done recently (September, 1872). Whether in doing the first portion I included or omitted the Cokes Tale of Gamelyn, I cannot now recollect. But it is of no importance, nor does it matter that a rhyme here and there may possibly have escaped my eye. I have no fear that any one who may go over the same ground will impugn the substantial accuracy of my statements.

TABLE I.—*Ew* words in Chaucer.

	salewe	(trans)mew	remewe	mewe, s.	(pur)sew	value	argue	due, adj.	eschieu	myscon-strew	glewe	stewe, s.	renew	truwe	Hugh	retenue	schewe	shrewe	thew= custom	fewe	hewe, vb.	dronkelewe	rewe= row, s.	new	hewe= colour	hewe= servant	(un)trewe	knew	(over)threw	rewe=pits	brewe	grew	blewe, adj.	drew	Lat.-u
salewe		2	1						1																										
(trans)mew	2								1																										
remewe	1										1																								
mewe, s.					1		1		1			2		1													1						1		
(pur)sew				1				1	1																		1	1						1	
value								1																											
argue				1					1																										
due, adj.					1	1			2															1			1								
eschieu	1	1		1	1		1	2		1			1											1											1
mysconstrew									1																										
glewe			1																																
stewe, s.				2																															
renew									1																										
truwe				1																															
Hugh																1																			
retenue															1																				
schewe																		4	1	4	1														
shrewe																	4		1	1		1	1												
thew = custom																	1	1																	
fewe																	4	1					1												
hewe, vb.																	1						1												
dronkelewe																		1																	
rewe = row, s.																		1		1	1														
newe								1	1																37		43	7	2	7	1	2	2		
hewe = colour																								17			17	6		5		2			1
hewe = servant																											1								
(un)trewe, adj.				1	1			1																43	17	1		6		12			1		1
knew					1																			7	6		6			3				1	1
(over)threw																								2											
rewe = pits																								7	5		12	3							
brewe																								1											
grew																								2	2										
blewe, adj.				1																				2			1								
drew					1																							1							
Lat.-u									1																1		1	1							

Now at the first glance it will be evident that some of these words are very exclusive in their social intercourse; for the words *shew, shrew, thew, few, hew, dronkelew, rew,* keep themselves entirely to themselves. There appears at once to be some truth in Palsgrave's distinction. But let us look at the whole of these words more in detail.

141 *Class 1. of French origin.* Class I. is of French origin.

1. Salewe, salue: Fr. saluer, O. Prov. and Span. saludar, Lat. and Ital. salutare.

2. Mewe, transmewe, remewe: O. Fr. muer, O. Prov. and Span. mudar, Lat. and Ital. mutare.

3. Mewe, s.: O. Fr. mue, Span. and Port. muda, Ital. muta, from the same root as the verb mew: see Wedgwood.

4. Sewe, swe, and pursew, pursue: O. Fr. suer.

5. Valew, value, valu: O. Fr. valoue, s., verb valoir, part. valu.

6. Argue, argewe: Fr. arguer, Lat. arguere.

7. Due, dewe: Fr. deü, deub, dû.

8. Eschieu, eschewe: O. Fr. esquiu, eschiu, eskiu, adj.; whence the verb eschever, eschiver, esquiver.

9. Mysconstrew: Fr. construire, Lat. construere.

10. Glewe: Fr. gluz, glu, Lat. gluten.

11. Stewe: O. Fr. estuve. Mr. Wedgwood thinks stewe fishpond to be a different word, which seems to me very doubtful.

12. Renewe: Kelham gives reneuf = renewed: Fr. neuf.

13. Trew, truwe = truce: Froiss. has unes trues: modern Fr. trève.

14. Hughe, Hewe, Huwe, Hwe: O. Fr. Huwe, Ger. Hugo.

15. Retenue, retenew: Fr. retenue.

142 *Class II. of Anglo-Saxon origin.* Class II. is of Anglo-Saxon origin.

1. Shewe, schewe, sschewe: A.S. sceáwian, sceáwigan, sceáwigean, &c.

2. Shrewe, scherewe, sherewe: A.S. screawa (or screáwa, judging by analogy.)

3. Thew = custom: A.S. þeáw, þeau.

4. Fewe: A.S. feáwe.

5. Hewe, vb.: A.S. heáwan.

6. Dronkelew, dronklew, drunkelewe: from A.S. druncen, and læwa (lǽwa?), a traitor = one who blabs secrets when intoxicated. The A.S. æw becoming *ew* in Chaucer finds an exact parallel in lewde from læwd, læwede, rhyming with i-thewde.

7. Rewe = row, s.: A.S. ræwa (rǽwa?) or rawa (ráwa?).

143 Class III. also of Anglo-Saxon origin. Class III. is also of Anglo-Saxon derivation.

1. New, newe, nwe: A.S. new, neow (neów?), niwe, nyw, niow (niów?).

2. Hew, hewe, hwe, hue, hiew, hiewe: A.S. hiw, heow (heów?), heaw, hiwe, hyew, hyw, hywe, heó.

3. Hewe: A.S. hiwa.

4. Trewe (and untrewe), trwe, treu, true, trowe: A.S. treów, tryw, triw, treu, trew.

5. Knew, knewe: A.S. cneów.

6. Threwe (and overthrewe): A.S. þreów is a form that does not, I believe, occur; but would be just analogous to cneów from cnáwan, seów from sáwan, and bleów from bláwan. (On the primary meaning of þráwan I have remarked in the Glossary to my ed. of Grossteste's Castle of Love, s. v. *Throw*.)

7. Rewe, rwe, rue: A.S. hreówan.

8. Brewe: A.S. briwan.

9. Grewe: A.S. greów.

10. Blewe: A.S. bleó.

11. Drewe, drew, drwe: A.S. dróh.

12. Latin words in -u (Jhesu, coitu) were in the same class.

144 Now of Class I. two words, "*mew* for a hauke and [else-

In Class I. *ew* = (yy). where] *glew*," are among those which Palsgrave sounded with the French *u*, which, if the above reasoning is sound, was (yy). This helps us to the whole class. The sound was (yy). But there are somewhat numerous imperfect rhymes. *Salew, mew*, vb., *transmew, remew, value, argue, mysconstrew, glew, stew, renew, truwe, Hugh, retenue*, rhyme only with this class: the rest offend as many as seven times in all out of twenty-eight—if that is many. Palsgrave puts "*rewe* an herbe" also in this class; and that is the Fr. *rue*, Lat. *ruta*.

145. In Class II. *ew* = (eu). Class II. in no instance rhymes with either of the others. What then was the sound? One of these words is *few*, in which, among others, Mr. Ellis (p. 139) discovers in an "anxiety to give prominence to the first element." But the A.S. forms all indicate that the first element was of importance; and that first element was *eá*,* or in one instance *á*, both of which I have above shown to have become (ee) by Chaucer's time. The diphthong therefore was very probably (eu) or (eeu), much like the Essex sound for *ow*, as in *cow*, *house*, (keeu), (heeus). And this is confirmed by Palsgrave's statement that the *ew* in *dewe, shrewe, Jewe*, was sounded like the Italian *eu*. That *dew* (Lat. ros) belongs to the same class, as Palsgrave makes it, is shown by the A.S. form deáw. As to *rewe*, a row (of which we also find the form *rowe* in some passages in some of the MSS., though not at the end of a verse), there seem to have existed two forms from a very early period.

146. In Class III. *ew* = (juu). Then we come to Class III, with words which in A.S. had *eu, iw, yw*, &c. The very diversity in spelling indicates the little importance of the first element as compared with Class II.; and there seems to be no reason why we should not here accept the traditional sound of (juu). And this is confirmed by Salesbury's authority; for this class includes the words *trewe* and *Jesu*, which Salesbury writes as *triw* and *tsiesuw*, and I cannot concede to Mr. Ellis, what every Welshman that I have consulted denies, that *iw* would represent to a Welshman either (yy) or any sound whatever that is at all familiar to English ears, other than that of the long English *u* (juu).

Palsgrave puts *true* and "a *clew* of threde" in the first of our Classes; but as to the latter which finishes no line in Chaucer, the A.S. orthography *cliwe* would assign it a

---

* I assume that in *sewewn* the accent belongs to the whole diphthong *eá*. But it may belong only to the *á*, the *e* serving the purpose of indicating the sibilant power of the *c*; then this is the form from which the modern *shew* would be derived. I apprehend the word, even in A.S., was pronounced in two ways, as it certainly was later. See § 168.

place with *new*, *hue*, &c., and as to *true*, both the A.S. spelling and Chaucer's rhymes show that Palsgrave's pronunciation was faulty.

The exceptions in this third Class are certainly not numerous. *New* forms 103 rhymes, only two of which are with the thinner *u*. *Hue* 68, all without exception with words of the same class. And so on as shown in the Table.

147 Objection from Salesbury. But Salesbury presents a difficulty which will need careful examination. In his Welsh representation of English sounds, he spells *virtue* with the same termination as *true* and *Jesu*, thus, *vertuw*; though in all probability this word, being of French derivation, would rhyme with *salew*, *value*, *due*, &c. in Chaucer's time, and would therefore *not* end in (juu). Salesbury moreover was nearly contemporary with Palsgrave, whose evidence we have just been hearing. Of course it is possible that Palsgrave's pronunciation was somewhat antiquated, and that even within half a century of his time the distinction which he observed might have become obsolete. The rhymes will no doubt help us. Here then is a second table to which the reader's attention is requested. It exhibits all the rhymes of this class (208 in number) that occur in Sir Philip Sidney's Poems, Heywood's Proverbs &c., and the First Book of the Faerie Queene. The words are classified according to derivation as before, except that some which refuse to drill with the rest have to be formed into an awkward squad by themselves.

§ 147] 'EW' WORDS. 109

TABLE II.—*Ew* words in Sidney, Heywood, Spenser.

148 *Palsgrave's distinctions had died out in the age of Queen Elizabeth.* What do we now discover? The sharp distinction that the other Table exhibited has quite disappeared here; and curiously enough the *cáw* class (*dew, hew, shew,** *few*), which in Chaucer rhyme exclusively among themselves, do not happen to do so even once throughout these poems, but everywhere with words of the other classes. The distinction which was so clear in Chaucer and familiar to Palsgrave is here entirely obliterated and forgotten, and the reasonable conclusion is that from the time of Queen Elizabeth these words have all been commonly pronounced as at the present day, though no doubt some orthoepical purists would try to fight against prevailing usage. But to judge from such authorities as those quoted by Mr. Ellis on p. 139, they contended for a distinction which etymology and ancient usage alike ignored.

149 *Another difficulty.* There remains yet one difficulty more. If so many of these words were sounded with a quasi-diphthong ending in (uu), and certain other words though differently spelt had the same sound, as *do, to, two,* how comes it—for it is the fact—that they never rhyme with these latter? For in Chaucer there is not one such rhyme, and only one (*you* with *do*) in these later poems. In Chaucer this may be partly accounted for by the fact that so many words in *-ewe* would (or at least might) sound the final *e*, so that *hewe* could no more rhyme with *do* than in modern French *heure* could rhyme with *bonheur*. But this does not fully solve the problem. Anglo-Saxon verbal preterites in *-eów*, had no additional syllable that could be rasped and pared down into an *-e*, so that when *-ewe* in *knewe, threwe,* &c. was written the final *e* was a mere addition to the eye, and never could have been sounded: at least such a corruption is in a high degree improbable. But we find in Chaucer the Latin *-u* rhyming not only with *knew* and *eschieu*, but also with *hewe* and *trewe*, with the final *e*; and yet it does not rhyme with *do* or *to*. I suppose

---

* Spenser uses this form as well as *show*. Sidney uses the latter alone, rhyming with *slow, low, grow,* &c.

the reason to be partly that the first element in the quasi-diphthongal (juu) seemed to make it an overmatch for the simple (uu), and partly that the poet was not content unless the rhyme satisfied not only the ear, but the eye, so far as the imperfectly settled orthography could satisfy it, just as Racine or Corneille will not make *moi* rhyme with *vois* or *voix*.

150 *But is the sound of (ə) of late introduction into our language? Almost identical with (v).* And now to return to the question whether the sound of (ə) as represented by the short *u* of *but* and *bun* existed in spoken English in Chaucer's time. The sound was probably rare then, for the grammarians, who carry us back as far as 1530, give no hint of it; yet I am not prepared to admit its non-existence. Clearly it exists now: it has come into the language at some time: the question is whether it is yet 500 years of age. It is obvious that it might be in occasional use just as we hear at times *soot* called (sət), and *put*, *foot*, and many more such pronounced with (ə) in provincial dialects—perhaps only in a few words, perhaps only among unfashionable and inexact speakers and not among "the better learned" (though any man then who could write as the Ellesmere or the Vernon MS. is written must have been among the educated men); and so it may have been rarer then than now: but did it exist at all in Chaucer's time?

In the first place I claim for (ə) all the arguments already adduced for a final (v), for the two sounds are so close to one another that it is doubtful whether they ought to be distinguished; they have almost one and the same sound appearing now in an open syllable, and now in a close one, and liable therefore to be modified by the consonant following. I shall henceforth use only (v).

151 *This sound existed in Early English, sometimes written u.* I have above hinted that such forms as *bysmoterud* (bəismutˑered?) and *rostud* in *Ha.*,* *offendude* in *L.*, *criud* in Dr. Morris's Old Eng-

---

* In the next few paragraphs and in the specimens which follow I use *E.* for the Ellesmere MS., *He.* for the Hengwrt, *Ca.* for the Cambridge, *Co.* for the Corpus, *P.* for the Petworth, *L.* for the Lansdowne, the six MSS. used for the Six-Text Chaucer; and *Ha.* for the Harleian, edited by Mr. Wright.

lish Miscellany, &c. look as if the *u* stood for the indistinct sound of (ɛ); but this cannot be insisted on. These terminations may be archaic forms straight in lineal descent from the A.S. *-ode* and *-od* (as in *lufode* and *gelufod*), with the (o) turned into the kindred (u).

But O.E. MSS. give us other forms not so easily disposed of: *tungus, aungelus, soulus, synnus,* as plurals; *godus, domus* (i.e. doom's), *worldus,* as genitives; *amongus, opure, broudun,* for *amanges, opere, brouden;* are readily found in glancing over a few pages of the Old English Miscellany. In my edition of the Castle of Love such forms are numerous: *goodschupe, opur, broþur, sugge* (= say), *undur, aftur, i-rud* (= advised), *þuncheth* (= seemeth), *hondrut,* &c. These examples are enough, though the list might easily be lengthened. My argument with regard to all these words is that etymology will not account for the sound of (u), the change of (e) into (u) cannot be shown to be probable, but its change into the indistinct (ɛ) is natural and simple to the English mouth, as hundreds (or shall I say thousands?) of English words bear witness.

152 *Sometimes (ɛ) was written with a.* But the sound may have existed without being always written with *u,* which certainly has no special fitness for representing it. In many instances it seems to have been written with *a,* as so often in modern English.* The Latin *Æmilia* shows what was the original vowel of the second syllable of *Emily;* but in Chaucer the name is commonly *Emelie* (em·elɔi), and the second syllable having become less sharp *Emaly* (em·ɛlɔi) results. Such is the form in *Ca.* continually; and few probably will suppose that the written *a* was there the symbol of the broad (a) rather than the simple (ɛ) which we still hear constantly in the mouths of careless speakers. The change in that case has been from (i) to (ɛ), which we also have in *destany, L.* and *P.,* for *destiny.* So (o) may become (ɛ, as when "*on*

---

* E.g. *tournament* and many more in *-ament, privacy* and others in *-acy, spectacle* and others in *-acle, probable* and all other hyperdissyllabic words in *-able, diaper, separate, tantamount, ragamuffin, barbarous, Jerusalem, L. Re.'s, Elizabeth,* &c. &c.; and see above § 128.

Goddes name" becomes "*a* Goddes name;" (e) may become (ĕ), as when the Dutch *taffetaf* gives us not only *tafeta*, L., but *taffata*, E., He., Ca., &c., and the A.S. *gemang, gelang, gelic*, &c. become in later times, *among, along, alike*, &c.; (AA), as when *all* (AAl) and *one* (oon) make *alone* (ĕloon); (u), as when Ca. gives us *wisdam* for *wisdom*, Ha. *martirdam*, and the Castell off Loue gives *wisdam*, *peuwedam*, and *wreccheddam*, the termination *-dóm* being akin to the Ger. *-thum*; (Ju), as when *Esculapius* appears in Co., P., and L., as *Escalapius*; and (ee), as when *sodein* gives us *sodanly*, L., *barein, baran*, L., *purtraiture, purtrature*, L. and P.

153 *Reasons against taking this short a as (a).*   It may naturally be asked, Why may not *a* in all these words have stood for (a)? I reply that there is only one sound into which all these are likely to have changed in careless speech. Our language, like the French,* has a thousand instances of changes of more clear and definite sounds into (ĕ): it is the vowel which is produced with least effort, and into which any of the others will degenerate through mere indolence of tongue. There is thus a sufficient reason why other vowels should become (ĕ), none why they should all become (a).

Nor are other indications wanting that some indistinct vowel was in use then as now. Such indications are found in the various ways in which one and the same word was written. When we find *marbel, marble, marbil, marbul; vilanye, vilonye; maladye, maledie; proper, propre, propur; tempel, tempul, temple; hamer, hamyr, hamure, hamur:* the reasonable conclusion is, not that the English did then, any more than their descendants do now, pronounce *malady* with the first two syllables as distinct as a Frenchman does in complaining of his *mal à la tête*, nor that so common a material as marble, or so common a tool as a hammer, was provided with four separate forms to its name; but that as neither had any one of the five vowel-symbols, nor

---

* Quem, quam, quod, quid, &c. have become que; ille, illum, illud, all ... ; amo, amat, amem, amet, all ... ; clementia, *Florence;* anima, *âme;* asinus, *âne*, &c.; and generally, the *-am* or *-em* of accusatives, and the *-us* and *-a* of adjectives, have all undergone the same change.

any combination of them, yet been appropriated to this sluggish sound, and orthography was as yet quite unsettled, one man chose to write the word one way, and another another. Mr. Ellis virtually acknowledges this, to the extent at least of writing the terminations -*ble*, -*ple*, &c. as (b'l), (p'l), &c.: I prefer (bǝl), (pǝl), and so on.

154 *In Anglo-Saxon also (v) was found.* This argument based on variety of spelling may, I think, fairly be urged as to Anglo-Saxon also; for there too, especially before liquids, the same word is found with different written vowels. Examples are— *hamar, hamer, hamor; weorpan, wurpan, wyrpan; weore, were, wore, wurce-an, wyre-an; regel, regol, regul; náðor, náðer, náðær, nanðr; mirht, myrhð, murhð;* * &c. But as to Anglo-Saxon we have not sufficient materials for forming a very confident judgment. Some of these differences may, it is obvious, be but dialectic varieties; but is there any reason why dialectic variety should specially affect vowels followed by *l* or *r*? It seems much more probable that these were only, or at least most commonly, different modes of writing the same spoken word.

155 *Oi words.* There remains yet one diphthong to be briefly discussed—that which we have in *noise, boy, oil,* &c. There exists in Chaucer a small class of such words, written as now with *oi* or *oy*: were they then sounded as now?

Mr. Ellis takes this *oi* or *oy* to have been always (ui)— that is the French *oui*—in Chaucer's time; which is the more remarkable as he supposes Englishmen of that period to have had no (i) or (ii) in their language, but only (*i*) or (*ii*).† As to the first element, there is some reason to think it was (u); namely, the authority of Gil (1621), who writes thus: " ü [= (uu)] antecedit i, in *ɜüint ioint* iunctura; in *brüil broile* torreo; *büil boile* coquo; in *büi boy* index anchorarius," &c.

---

* If I am right in supposing these three forms to have been all (mrxth) or (muth), we can easily suppose that the adjective which is now *merry*, but formerly very commonly written with *u, murie,* had the same vowel; and then Chaucer's rhyme of *Mercurie* and *murie* is clear, each word ending in (uri).

† So that *wine* would be sounded not as we now sound *ween*, but as *win* is sounded when prolonged in singing.

156. *The o in OI probably = (u).*

There are indeed two objections to this view. The first is found in certain statements of grammarians which are apparently adverse to that of Gil. Butler (1633) says: "*Oi* in *boy* we sound, as the French do, *woë;* bois, soit, droict, as bwoes, swoet, drwoet;" and similarly Erasmus directs the Greek *οι* to be sounded like the French *oi* in *moi, toi, soi, foi, loi, roi;* while Meigret, Pelletier, Livet, all make the first sound in the French *oi* to be *o*. Hart, Smith, and Salesbury, all seem to mean the same, making the diphthong nearly or quite (*oi*). These authorities are mostly quoted by Mr. Ellis, pp. 130 to 133. The conclusion to which they seem to point is, that the sound was a diphthong hard to analyse, the first element of which was either (o) or (wo) or (u), and the second was either (*i*) or (e).

Secondly, we may appeal to the orthography of the MSS. of Chaucer. *O* sounded as (uu) is found, I think, exclusively in words purely English; but it seems to stand for the short (u) in some words of French derivation, in which, however, it often varies in writing into *u*, such as *corteis* or *curteis, doseyn* or *duszein, norysche* or *nurysche, contree* or *cuntree;* and in most if not all of these the traditional pronunciation is with (o), which no doubt has passed through an (u) stage. But in all the *oi* words that I can find in our seven MSS., I find only a single instance out of hundreds where one of these *oi* words has *u*, and then it is not *ui* or *uy:* the word is *puyvant* in *L*. alone, Prol. 352. All the other words—*oil, ointment, boil, broile, cloister, oyster, royal, royally, moist, point, broided, joynant, quirboily, joy, noise, choice, voice,* &c.—are spelt with *oi* or *oy* (except occasional by-forms such as *real* and *breided*).

On the other hand two considerations, when added to Gil's distinct and positive assertion, seem to overbear these objections. First, a rhyme such as *coy, Loy* (Cant. Ta. Prol. ll. 119, 120), needs explanation; for the first syllable of *Loy* in almost every form which the word has assumed—*Ludwig, Ludovicus, Louis, Lewis,* &c.—apparently contains the sound of (u): indeed if we could believe that the modern French pronunciation of *Louis* is precisely what it was 500 years ago, and that the true French sound was precisely reproduced by English lips when such words were, 500 years ago, borrowed into our language, we must then conclude that Chaucer sounded his *Loy* with the *oy* the modern (not *oui* after all, but) *ouï;* and we cannot but believe that the sound *approximated* to this. Secondly, in several of these words a written *u* remains even now, as in *huile, huître, nuire, bouillir, brouiller, gargouille,* &c. Confirming this, traces of the Latin original with *u* appear here and there in the old forms, as *juindre* from *jungere, puindre* from *pungere,* &c.

On the whole I cannot believe the sound to have been

157 *The true sound probably (ui) or (ue).* exactly either that of the French *oui* or that of our modern *oi.* The balance of evidence seems to be in favour of (u*i*) or (u*e*). The second element must be (*i*) or (*e*) rather than the thinner, finer (i), for two reasons: the first, that the repeated comparison of the English sound with the French by Palsgrave and the other grammarians must be interpreted by the aid of Meigret's *oé* as more accurately representing the French *oi,* and (*i*) or (*e*) is nearer to *è* than (*i*) is; and the second, that it can scarcely be supposed to be the long (ii), and the short (i) occurs in English in no close syllables, while both (*i*) and (*ee*) are common in final open syllables, as in *sit* (s*i*t), *hill* (h*i*l), *pin* (p*i*n), *happy* (ħæp'*i*), *manly* (mæn·l*i*), *may* (m*ee*), *say* (s*ee*). Perhaps also, for the first element, the true sound had the close *o.* But all this is little more than conjecture, and it seems impossible to arrive at certainty.

I have now touched on the principal points on which I

158 *Conclusion.* decline to accept, or care to dispute, Mr. Ellis's views: a few words in conclusion and my task is done.

I fear some expressions in the preceding pages may seem to indicate a degree of confidence in the conclusions arrived at which I do not in reality entertain. On many points I certainly do feel confident: on others I am much more firmly convinced that Mr. Ellis's views are unsound than that my own are unassailable. The probability certainly is that as we are, I believe, the first explorers in this hitherto untrodden country, we both have strayed here and there into bogs and quagmires, and have neither of us fully succeeded in finding the precious nuggets and opening up the rich veins of ore which our ambition has sought.

We both have been writing on *Early English;* yet so tempting have been the adjacent fields in which discovery seemed possible that we have ventured far beyond. And for myself the further I have ventured, the less firm the ground has seemed under my feet. I can readily imagine that the progressive study of the Early German dialects may show what at present seems to me incredible—that a thousand years ago the whole population would speak of (miin wiin), and then some portions only of the population came somehow to say (mɔin wɔin), while other portions, without any apparent difference of internal instinct or tendency, or of external influence of any kind, stuck to the old sounds. In like manner I can conceive that further investigation, and in particular the systematic course of inquiry on which the English Dialect Society has entered, may show my conclusions on at least some points of A.S. pronunciation to be either doubtful or certainly incorrect.* Possibly too even the tendency-theory, which at present I look at with grave suspicion, may be so dressed up that it cannot but be accepted. But coming down to later times, where the evidence is at once so abundant and so varied, I am somewhat more sanguine as to the general acceptance by scholars of most of the views here propounded.

* I earnestly hope our students of *aizizi* will also be students of *dialects*, and investigate with care the nature not only of the premises from which they draw their conclusions, but also of the connexion between the premises and the conclusions drawn. If for instance any investigator of dialects who is also a strong believer in the tendency-theory should light upon some pronunciation which seems to him to have been developed from some other supposed earlier pronunciation, let him not rush too inconsiderately to conclusions as to Chaucer's English or as to Anglo-Saxon. Whatever really can be proved, let it be proved by evidence adduced; let it not merely be asserted. It is very easy to say "Here we have in the pronunciation of these villages a dialect in the very act of transition;" but it is not so easy to prove that the ancestors of those same villages spoke otherwise two hundred or two thousand years ago. And if the

In any case it must be allowed that Mr. Ellis's voluminous work, as an immense repertory of a certain class of facts, will always be of great value to the students of the subjects of which it treats.

fact of a changed pronunciation can be really proved (as no doubt it can in some instances), there yet remains the question, What is the degree of rapidity —and how can you *prove* the degree of rapidity—with which the change has taken place? Has it taken place in a few generations of mankind, or has it required a quasi-geological period to complete it?

While I have positive evidence that 240 years ago, as now, the word *Thames* was sounded *Tems*, and *Thomas, Tomas*, and *disdeign, reign, flegme, signe*, did not sound the *g*—so Butler (1633) informs us; that 300 years ago the distinction of the surd and sonant *th* was, in every word that Hart gives, exactly the same as at present; that 400 years ago *hard, correk, falowship, prevaly, deligent*, were written forms to represent the Scotch sounds then, as they do very accurately now, of *heard, correct, fellowship, privily, diligent*—see above, p. 8; that 500 years ago *England* was (at least sometimes) called *Ingland*— see below, note on l. 16; that 800 or 1000 years ago *meny, many, mony = multi*, were forms (I speak of the first syllable) that existed side by side—see Bosworth—just as in England, Ireland, and Scotland they do now;—I cannot but look with suspicion on any theory which represents our language, or any language, as in such a furious state of ebullition and fermentation that, could our great grandfathers start up from their graves, we and they would scarcely be able to understand one another's speech.

That language does undergo changes no man in his senses can doubt; but, so far as the *evidence* goes, the change, in my judgment, resembles, not some violent chemical action, but rather the gradual and slow disintegration of the limestone or the granite of the everlasting hills.

APPENDIX.

It seems desirable to add a passage or two from the Canterbury Tales, by way of specimen of the manner in which I suppose the English of Chaucer to have been pronounced. But besides the general inquiry what sound or sounds were usually represented by each letter in Early English, this whole investigation is, as elsewhere remarked, to a great extent the study of individual words; and it will therefore be necessary to inquire with some degree of minuteness concerning a good many words whence they came, what various forms they have possessed in our language and in others, and what sounds writers later than Chaucer have assigned to them, thus to determine, if possible, how each one was sounded both by itself and in contact with others (a distinction of which Mr. Ellis has quite lost sight): this I have attempted to do in the foot notes.

Here bygynneth the Book of the tales of Caunterbury.

Whan that Aprille with hise schoures soote

1. It is not for the sake of differing that I differ from Mr. Ellis on no fewer than twelve points in this first line!

—whæn: A.S. *hwænne*. There was also the form with a thinner vowel, *hwenne*, but none with *a*.

—dhæt: A.S. þæt or ðæt. There is no form with *a*. As to the initial *th*, A.S. does not help us. Indeed if only one A.S. form existed, I should base no argument upon it, believing that þ and ð were not distinguished as in Icelandic, but only different forms of the same letter, some scribes preferring one and some the other. In Orm. we have only þ, in the Hatton MS. of Greg. Past. only ð. In this word, and in *widh*, I follow tradition, finding no safer guide. But we can go back with certainty for three centuries at least, for Hart (1569) distinguishes the sonant *th* from the surd, and the distinction is, I think, without exception throughout his book precisely the same as in this 19th century: at least I have not noticed a single word that he writes with ð, which we do not now sound with the sonant (dh).

—apr*i*l: both the metre and the accent of the French original (itself derived from that of the Lat. *Aprīlis*) show the accent to have been on the second syllable. Also, every one of the Six MSS. (as well as *Ha.*) has *ll* after the *i*, from which I conclude that the *i* was short. Compare *croppes*, *sonne*, *ironne*, &c. I certainly do not mean that in the MS. of Ch. the same rule as in Orm. is habitually followed; far from it. But where there is so marked an agreement, and when in a large number of instances we have other and independent evidence that the vowel is short, the conclusion from such induction is very clear.

—Mr. Ellis supposes that in this line the first measure is defective. I prefer to believe that even in Chaucer's time the choriambus was often substituted for the diiambus, and that this verse begins with a choriambus (_ ◡ ◡ _), the omitted syllable being in the middle of the verse where a pause compensates for it, thus:

$$\_\ \cup\ \cup\ \_\ (\cup)\ \_\ \cup\ \cup\ \_$$

or

The rhythm of the beginning of the line seems to me to be precisely that of Milton's—

> *Ser'vant of God'*, well done, well hast thou fought!

where the last four syllables also form a choriambus; and compare Shakspeare's

> *Mer'ciful Heav'en!*
> Thou rather with thy sharp and sulphurous bolt
> *Splitt'st' the unwedge'*able and gnarled oak
> *Than' the soft myr'tle:* O but man, proud man,
> *Drest' in a lit'*tle brief authority, &c.

—hize: Mr. Ellis omits the *h*. But when spelling was unsettled, and therefore very largely phonetic, if the corrupt and slovenly pronunciation of the 19th century had already come into vogue, we should certainly see proof of the fact

SPECIMENS. 121

Hii1 bíginˑeth dhᴇ buuk ᴇv dhᴇ tæælˑez ᴇv kAAntˑᴇɹberi.

whæn dhæt aprílˑ widh ʜíz'ᴇ shəurˑez suut

in *is* for *his*, and so on, very commonly in the MSS. I do not remember to have met with a single instance of the kind, and therefore confidently believe that the *h* used to be as scrupulously pronounced as it is still by even uneducated Irishmen and Scotchmen in their English.

—ʜíz'ᴇ: As to the *z* as sign of the genitive, partly I fall back on tradition, knowing for certain, from Hart (1569) Bullokar (1580) that the *s* has been so sounded for the last three centuries. Both of these authorities write *hiz*. But see further in note on *lordes*, l. 47.

—shəurˑez: this word, though its O.N. form is *skúr*, is supposed by Mr. Welgwood to be akin to the Ger. *schauer*. Engl., Ger., and Du. words in (əu) commonly have *ú* (uu) in O.N.

—shəurˑez: for the *z* as sign of the plural, I again rest partly on tradition, and the authority of Hart and Bullokar for three centuries, finding in Bullokar *bemz* (beams), *wyuz* (wives), *thôz*, and in Hart *premisez*, *aulwez* (always), *vertiuz*. But there is an additional argument. I venture to think, in opposition to Dr. Latham, that the normal sibilant with which the plural is formed in modern English is not *s* but *z*, and that for two reasons: first, because of the effect it often produces on a consonant preceding, changing *f*, *s* (in some words), and the surd *th* into *v*, *z*, and the sonant *th*, as *wife wives*, *house houses*, *path paths*; second, because when the singular ends in a sound which the surd *s* could as easily follow as the sonant *z*, the plural yet does not take *s* but *z*, as *trees* (triiz), *hills* (Hilz), *pins* (pinz).

—shəurˑez: the vowel of the plural termination was in A.S. *a*, as in *smiðas*: but in modern English it has thinned down into (e) whenever it is sounded, as in (tshʉɹtshez), (boksez), (brídzhez). I have remarked in § 151 that plurals sometimes appear in -*us*, which seems to indicate the obscure sound of (ʉs); but in the great majority of instances the form is -*es*, or, thinner still, -*is* or -*ys*, so that the sound of (ʉs) can have been only rare and exceptional.

suut: for the (uu) see p. 39. As to the final vowel, *if* it was sounded, I believe the sound to have been (ᴇ); see § 128. Professor Child has truly remarked that "it is a question which may be called at least a *difficult* one to solve, whether the *e* in many cases was absolutely dropped, or only slightly pronounced;" and I fully agree with Mr. Ellis that "Chaucer *may* have used an *e* final in poetry, which was unknown in common speech." These "difficult" questions I am content to leave in the able hands which have already been dealing with them, not having any very strong opinion on the subject, though somewhat inclined to side with Mr. Payne (Essays on Chaucer, No. IV., published by the Chaucer Society.) The argument that has decided me not to print any final vowel, is that if every *e* was sounded at the end of Chaucer's lines, the number of weak rhymes becomes excessive. Apart from these, we find only three weak rhymes in the first 100 lines — *corṣ.s, pilgrimages, stronds londes, sensyble tables*; but with these no fewer than 35 out of the 50 pairs of lines form weak rhymes. It is hard to believe that Chaucer could have intended this. And there is yet this farther to be said (though I

The droghte of March | hath perced to the roote

shall seem scarcely to be *leaving* the matter in the able hands alluded to); if the final *e* was habitually sounded, we should not find so very frequently as we do that in the same passage one MS. has it and another omits it. A mere glance at the Six-Text Chaucer shows at once lines ending in different MSS. with *walle wal, schone schon, ymaginynge ymagynyng, bouȝe bough, foreste forest*. And again, we find words with the final *e* rhyming with others without it, as *forest beste, þrafte laft, ymaked nakede*.

2. dhʋ : compare top of p. 64 with § 130. Palsgrave, a little more than a century after Chaucer's time, assigns to the vowel in *the* the sound of the Italian *i* (Lesclar., pp. 3 and 6). That sound it preserves to this day when the word stands alone or before a vowel; but we sound it (dhʋ) before a consonant, and this usage had probably already set in at the period when *Rome* (see p. 96) could be made to rhyme with *to me*. A difficulty is presented by the fact that Hart always writes *the* as ẟe, making no distinction whether a vowel followed or a consonant; but the single form ẟinstruments is sufficient to show that the sharp (ii) might in his time even before a vowel be pronounced so obscurely that it could easily be elided, and that obscure sound will be (ʋ).

—drokȝcht : it seems necessary to add a few remarks to what has been said in the preceding pages (§ 132) on the *o* words.

Besides the two classes of *o* words in Chaucer dealt with in §§ 46 to 56, there are several others, which it may be worth while to specify in detail. They are—1st, those that in Chaucer sometimes are spelt with *o*, sometimes with *u*, as *scholde, scholdre, tonge, corteis*, &c.; 2nd, those that always have *o* in Chaucer, but are now always pronounced with (ɔ), as *boket, bokeler, month, yong*, &c.; 3rd, those that begin with *wo*, now (wu), as *wolf, wolde*, &c.; 4th, those that begin with *wo*, now (wɔ), *wonne, worthy*, &c.; 5th, those that have *o* in Chaucer, and have (oo) now, as *open, spoken*, &c.; 6th, those that have (o) now, as *holt, holpen*, &c., the *o* in these words being followed by *l*; 7th, those that in A.S. had *a* (or *o*), as *hond, lond, strong*, &c., the *o* in these being followed by *nd* or *ng*; 8th, those that had *o* in A.S., which the Orm. shows to have been short, and which is still (ɔ); 9th, others with *o* from the O.N. or French, as *dog, mortel, morsel*, &c.

We have, however, a simpler but important division into those which can be shown in any stage to have contained an *u* sound, and those which cannot.

Believing that *o* in many words stood for a long (uu), I can have no difficulty in believing it to have stood at times for a short (u), and that in probably all words which at any time had (u). On the other hand, where there is no distinct evidence that a word at any time had (u), the fair conclusion is that Chaucer sounded it with some *o* sound.

Now Mr. Ellis teaches that Chaucer knew only two such sounds, (o) and (oo); and he may be right; yet it is singular that neither of these is at present a recognized English sound at all, the former being, according to Mr. Ellis's Key to Palæotype, exemplified in the French *homme*, the second in the Italian *nomo*. (It is always with the greatest reluctance and with a feeling akin to

dhʊ drokʒht ʊv maɹtsh Hæth pers'ed tu dhʊ ruut,

---

trepidation that I venture to differ from Mr. Ellis on a point of pure phonetics, for I certainly know no one whose accuracy of ear equals or approaches his. But when on p. 226—in the sentence on which my already-printed § 132 is based—he claims the sound of (o) for *cross* and *gone*, this seems to me a sentence written *per σφάλμα*. To my ear those words are (krɔs) or (krʌs) and (gɔn) or (gʌn), and the true Italian *o aperto*, either long or short, has no existence in our language.) Undoubtedly (*o*) or (*oo*) is now our long English *o*, as in the ordinary pronunciation of *go home* (go ɦoom); and it does not follow because the early orthoepists may have simply *failed to notice* the difference between this (*o*) or (*oo*) and the French (o) or (oo), as in *robe* and *rôle*, *notre* and *nôtre*, that there was no such difference. The sound may have been the common English sound 500 years ago, as it is at present; and there being no evidence to the contrary, I must believe it was so.

Then there is another sound of *o*, which it has now in all close syllables that end in a mute, and often also before a liquid, as in *not*, *rock*, *for*, in palæotype (nɔt), (rɔk), (fɔɹ). It is almost or quite this sound that we hear in the German *kopf*, It. *sotto*, Fr. *donner*, Du. *bottel*, Span. *torre*, &c., and it is so commonly regarded throughout all Western Europe as simply "the short *o*"—in Italy alone, I believe, the two short *o*s are commonly distinguished—that we may reasonably expect to find like inaccuracy in the observations of our early phonologists. Accordingly, when I find Butler (1633) affirming that *cost* and *coast*, *for* and *fore*, "differing from themselves in quantity, have yet the same sound," I do not feel convinced that his observation deserves implicit reliance, especially as in the latter of his pairs of words the distinction of (fɔɹ) and (fooɹ) is not easy to make in pronouncing a sentence, but that of (fɔɹ) and (fooɹ) or (foɹ) is very easy.

Moreover I have adduced (§§ 119 to 121) at least plausible reasons for believing (ʌʌ) as in *all*, *tall*, *saw*, *raw*, to be a genuine and ancient English sound; and if those reasons are accepted, it must be admitted to be probable that the shorter (ʌ), as in *want*, *what*, *august*, should also be ancient; but this sound differs scarcely or not all from (ɔ). *What* rhymes perfectly with *hot*, the *-ant* of *want* has precisely the same sound as the *-ont* of *contrary*, *august* sounds its *aug-* a little longer than the *-og* of *log* or *dog*, but the sound to my apprehension is absolutely the same in quality. Therefore, given (ʌʌ) in Chaucer, (ɔ) follows.

In the particular word before us, the guttural seems to require the open (ɔ).

—drokʒht : kʒh is the palæotype mode of representing the guttural heard in the German *au-h*. That the guttural was not yet lost is rendered highly probable by the fact that it is never omitted in writing (just as I have argued on the *h* of *his*). The exact nature of the guttural depends of necessity, as in German, on the vowel that precedes.

—drokʒht : I believe with Mr. Ellis that a final *e* was commonly cut off before a vowel following, as here the final *e* of *droghte* disappears before the *of*.

—ʊv : Hart bears witness that for more than three centuries the *f* in *of* has been (v). The word by itself would probably be pronounced (ɔv); but people

And bathed euery veyne | in swich licour
Of which vertu | engendred is the flour
Whan Zephirus eek | with his swete breeth   5
Inspired hath | in euery holt and heeth
The tendre croppes | and the yonge sonne
Hath in the Ram | his half[e] cours yronne

500 years ago were no more likely to make a special effort to keep the open vowel on a mere particle requiring no emphasis, and with no pause before it, than we do now. We must not forget that the English of Chaucer's time was the language employed in all the familiar intercourse and rapid speech of daily life.

—Hæth: Mr. Ellis gives (Hath), which may be heard in the West of England; but the A.S. *hafð* points to the still prevailing sound as also the most ancient, and therefore likely to have been the common one in Chaucer's time.

3. and: perhaps (ænd) as at present, for Bosworth gives an A.S. form *ænde*, as well as the more usual *and*.

—bæædh·ed: in Orm. we find the *e* of the past participle was apparently distinct and short (see § 127), and such is the prevailing pronunciation at the present day; therefore also probably throughout the intervening centuries.

—ev·eri: Mr. Ellis writes ev·rii; but the termination seems to be the same as in the A.S. *æghwile*, in which the vowel was most probably short.

—li̇kaur: here also Mr. Ellis writes li̇i, but with the well marked accent on the second syllable it is far more likely according to our English mode of pronunciation that the first syllable would be shortened. The final *r* Mr. Ellis takes to have been fully trilled. That orthoepists earlier than Ben Jonson *failed to notice* or describe the non-vibrant *r*, is no proof that the sound did not exist: the art of phonologic observation was not, and could not be, perfected all at once. National usage too, and even local usage, continues unchanged for centuries in France; for both Palsgrave and (I think, speaking from memory) Erasmus bear witness to the peculiar sound of the Parisian *r*: why must we, on mere negative evidence, assume great changes to have taken place in our English pronunciation?

—vǣn: the final *e* elided.

—As to metre this line has a tribrach for the second foot, with the ictus on the second syllable as in Latin and Greek iambics:

Compare from Shakespeare,

The arm'd *rhinoc'e·*ros or the Hyrcan tiger;

and from Milton,

Celes·*tial spir'its* in bondage, nor th' abyss;

and this with two tribrachs,

Nay if *the dev'il hath giv'en* the·e proofs for sin—*Shakspeare.*

4. veattyy·: there can be little doubt that the *u* of *vertu* would be sounded like that of *salu*·, *valu*, *retour*, on which see §§ 141 and 144.

—endzhen·dread: was there a *d* sound in the so-called soft *g* in Early English? Everybody knows that all our words that contain this sound (with perhaps the single exception of *gib* from the the O.N. *gip*) are from the

and bæædh·ed ev·er*i* veen *i*n sw*i*tsh l*i*kəɹɹ·,
ɔv wh*i*tsh veɹtjyy· endzhen·dɹɹd *i*z dhɐ flɔuɹ;
whæn zef*i*rus iik w*i*dh H*i*z swiit·ɐ breeth.   5
*i*nspəir·ed Hæth *i*n ev·er*i* Holt and heeth
dhɐ ten·drɐ krɔp·ez, and dhɐ juq·ɐ sun
Hæth *i*n dhɐ ram H*i*z Half kəu·ɹs *i*run,

French: the question therefore is virtually, was the soft *g* in Early French sounded as we now sound it in English? I believe in Early French both *ch* and *j* and the soft *g* were sounded, not as (sh) and (zh) as now, but as (tsh) and (dzh), as we sound them in *chair* and *ginger*. In addition to what Mr. Ellis has written (pp. 314, 315), I may refer to the Mediæval Greek ὁμάτζιον for *homage*, and Πλατζαφλώρια for Blancheflеur, and to *orge* as derived from *hordeum*.

—endzhen·dɹɹd: for the *-dred* see note on *chambres*, l. 28.

—*i*z: the *s* in *is* has been sounded as *z* for at least three centuries *teste* Hart's *iz*.

5. On *ok* and *stote* as (ii) words see §§ 97 and 99; and on *breeth* and *heeth*, l. 6, as (ee) words see §§ 84 and 101 to 105. Of *breeth* Ca. gives the form *breth*, indicating possibly, even when that MS. was written, a tendency to shorten the vowel as it is shortened now: see top of p. 76. *Breeth*, as it stands, seems to represent just the same sound as we now give to the word but with the vowel a little prolonged.

—swiit·ɐ: the final vowel sounded because of the determinative *his* preceding. As to the quality of the vowel as an adjective termination, the fact that it is so commonly elided before a vowel following, and, as there is reason to believe (see note on *sote*, l. 1), often dropped altogether, makes it almost certain that it could not have been a clear, sharply-pronounced vowel.

6. Holt: A.S. *holt*, and the word in no stage is written with *u*. On negative evidence the existing pronunciation seems likely to have been the ancient one.

7. ten·drɐ: all of the MSS. here have the final *e*, which needs to be pronounced after the determinative *the*: the word is, in fact, contracted from *tendre*. Were it undeclined, it would probably be pronounced (tend·ɐɹ): see note on *chambres*, l. 28.

krɔp·ez: the double *p* indicates a short vowel, which before the explosive mute is most probably the same as we now sound in the word.

juq·ɐ: the adjective had two forms in A.S., *geong* and *giung*, besides others of less importance. The former of these,—unless it should be more correctly *góng*, which would probably be sounded (juuq),—is now represented by the West Country *yong*, rhyming with *long* and *strong*; the latter is nearer in form to the Ger. *jung*. That *young* had "*ou* pro *u*" we learn from Cooper, as late as 1685, and Gil sounds the vowel just as in *wuman*, *wul*, *bush*, *wud*.

sun: Butler (1633) and Gil (1621) both give *son* and *sun* (as we now write them) the same sound, namely, with the same (u) as that of *wuman*, &c.

8. ram or rɐm: A.S. *ram*, *ramm*; yet the change which the word has undergone may have been effected by Chaucer's time.

And smale foweles | maken melodye
That slepen al the nyght | with open eye   10
So priketh hem nature in hir corages
Thanne longen folk | to goon on pilgrimage [s]
And Palmeres | for to seken straunge strondes
To ferne halwes | kowthe in sondry londes
And specially | from euery shires ende   15

—hAlf: Gil's *hálf* proves that at least two centuries and a half ago the *a* in this word was sounded as the *a* or *aw* in *walk* (I give his spelling), *wäl*, *fäl*, *läu*, *drä*, *strä*, &c.; as Butler also (1633) and Cooper (1685) teach.

—*P.* has *halfe*. From *E* Mr. Furnivall gives half[e], but the other four MSS. have no *e*, and I have followed their lead. If *half* is the true reading, it follows that Chaucer in this line allows a pause instead of the short syllable of the fourth foot, and does not always keep the final *e* after a determinative.

—*irun*: A.S. *urnen*, Ger. *geronnen*. The *u* points to the sound of (u) which the rhyme demands.

9. smAAl·e or smæxl·e: see §§ 73 and 75.

—fou·əlez: the word is trisyllabic in *E.* and *He.*, so that the second foot of this line is a tribrach, as in l. 3.

—mel·odəi: see §§ 17 and 90.

10. AAl: see § 73.

—ni*k*ht: the vowel is short in the Orm., where the form is *nihht*: when it became long, as at present sounded, I have failed to discover. Probably when the guttural went out of use.

—*oop·*en: almost all our pure English words that now have a long (oo) had *á* in A.S.: this word is one of the very few exceptions, the earliest form being like the present one *open*. From the A.S. spelling I conclude that it was sounded (ɔp·en), as it still is in the West of England. Orm. shows that both sounds existed in his time, writing the adjective as *opénn* and the verb as *oppnenn*.

11. Hur: I follow here the reading of *Ca.*, *Ce.*, *P.*, *L.*, and *Ha.* in preference to that of *E.* and *He.* which give *hir*. For the sound, see note on l. 32.

—kuræædzh·ez: it admits of doubt whether the *-age* in this class of words has a short *a*, so that they would rhyme with the modern *badge* and *Madge*, or a long one, as I have assumed in § 75. On the whole, as the vowel is always sounded long in the French *courage*, &c., and these words in Chaucer's time had not been very long in the language, it is more likely that the syllable was long in English also.

—kuræædzh·ez: Mr. Ellis writes (koo). But it is the *general* rule of our language to shorten every syllable except the accented one; indeed exceptions, such as *almighty* (AAlməiti), are not numerous. Moreover in the French, if we appeal to the modern pronunciation, we find that the stress of the voice is on the *cou*, but yet it is pronounced short (ku). This *o* is most likely to have been (u), as in French the form *curáge* was the more ancient.

12. dhæn·e: A.S. *þanne*, an old accusative singular. This form in *E.* and *He.* gives us an anapæst in the first foot, admissible also in Greek iambics.

SPECIMENS.

and smAAl·ʋ fəu·elez mæækˑen melˑodəi,
dhæt sliipˑen AAl dhʋ nikht widh oopˑen əi— 10
soo prikˑeth Hem natjyyr in Heɹ kuræædzhˑez- ;
dhænˑʋ ləqˑen fəlk tu goon ən pilgrimæædzhˑez,
and palˑmiirez fəɹ tu siikˑen strAAndzhˑʋ strandˑez,
tu ferˑnʋ Halʲwez kəuth in sundˑri lAndˑez ;
and spesˑiAləi frəm evˑeri shəirˑez iind 15

—folk: there seems to be no evidence of the antiquity of the custom of not sounding the *l* in this word, though Butler (1633) tells us that in his time the *l* was dropped in *calf, half, salve, calves, walk, talk, Halkin, Malkin, alms, almond,* and many other words. As all the best MSS. exhibit the *l*, it was most probably sounded.

—pilgrimæædzhˑez: *E.* has the singular *pilgrimage*.

13. palˑmiirez: *palmere* is the modern Fr. *paumier*, and all such words (see § 92, in which this word ought to have been mentioned) rhyme with *here*, not with *there* (see p. 67). *Co.* spells the word *palmeris*, and this by no means infrequent form of the plural termination makes it clear that though the original *-as* became thinned down into *-es* and *-is*, it did not commonly change the vowel into the obscure (ʋ). See § 153.

—siikˑen: see § 97. Independently of the rhymes which this word forms, that the *e* is long may be safely concluded from its being doubled in the three MSS., *He., L.,* and *Ha.*

—strAAndzhˑʋ: Mr. Ellis for this (AA) writes (au), which he would pronounce as in the Ger. *haus;* but where does the (u) element come from? See below on *Caunturbury,* l. 16. (On p. 144, when quoting Sir Thomas Smith, Mr. Ellis seems quite to misunderstand Smith's protest against the then prevailing mode of sounding αὐδάω: what Smith objected to was the Modern Greek pronunciation of αὐδάω as ἀ-tδάω.)

14. Halʲwez: possibly Hælˑwez; but no derivative of *hálig* with a short *æ* appears in A.S. The Orm. does not help beyond showing that the vowel is short, the form being *hallʒenn*.

—sunˑdri: that the A.S. word had *u* in the first syllable, and that the modern form is *sundry*, seem to be sufficient reasons for reading the *o* as (u), as in *ʋonge sonne,* l. 7. On the (*i*) see on *hoolʲy,* l. 17.

15. spesˑiAləi.: that the *s* in such words was not sounded as *sh* up to the 16th century may perhaps be inferred from its not being mentioned; but the strongest argument seems to me to be one which Mr. Ellis has overlooked, namely that Hart had a special symbol for (sh) and does not use it in writing *observacion, derivasion, nasion,* &c.

spesˑiAləi: for the pronunciation of adjectives in *-al* down to the seventeenth century, see § 120, foot note † 3, p. 89.

spesˑiAləi: for the *-ly,* see note on *sleethˑly,* l. 30.

shəirˑez, perhaps shiirˑez: the word *shire* undoubtedly has an exceptional pronunciation as (shiir), and as in Chaucer it nowhere ends a line except in l. 350, rhyming with *sire* which does not, I believe, occur elsewhere, the argument of § 109 will not apply to it.

Of Engelond | to Caunturbury they wende
The hooly blisful martir for to seke
That hem hath holpen | whan þat they were seeke
Bifil that | in that seson on a day

—iind·e, and wiind·e l. 16: in the word *fiend* we preserve the sound which I believe *friend* (which habitually rhymes with it in Chaucer) to have formerly possessed. But *ende* in Chaucer repeatedly rhymes with *friend*; in the Orm. it has a long vowel (endenn); and Cooper, 1685, expressly records *eend* as belonging to the "barbara dialectus," which doubtless means an old and now unfashionable pronunciation. In like manner *wende* continually rhymes with *ende* in Chaucer, and this too has ē in Orm. (wendenn), except in the past tense (wennde), where the *e* is short as in the modern *went*.

16. *iq·gelAnd*: possibly the (iq·) should be (eq·) as written. But both *Co.* and *L.* write *Ing·*, and this is certainly an ancient pronunciation of the word. Jones (1704) so sounds *England*, *English*, *Englefield*, and Bullokar (1580) writes *Inglish*. Our two MSS. however are yet higher authority. And their evidence is corroborated by that of the MS. of Lawrence Minot, assigned by Mr. Wright "to the earlier part of the 15th cent., probably to the reign of Henry V." In this MS. the common forms are *Ingland* and *Ingliss*. (See Wright's Political Poems and Songs, vol. i. pp. 64, 70, 78, &c.) Where there are such exceptional pronunciations, evidences of their longevity abound on every hand.

—*iq·gelAnd*: the hard *g* was most probably sounded in *Angle* (as we still sound it in that word, and in *jangle*, *wrangle*, *tangle*—not *ang·l*, &c. as in the Ger. *Angel*); and therefore also in *Engelond*.

—*kAAnt·uaburi*: 1st syllable. Here five of our MSS. write *Caunt·*, only *L.* and *Ha.* have *Cant·*. In l. 801 *Co.* and *P.* also have *Cant·*. This syllable Mr. Ellis sounds (kaunt) distinctly introducing an (u) sound. Not only is the spelling *Cant·*, opposed to this, but the question of necessity arises, Where did this (u) come from? There seems to have been only a simple vowel when Cæsar wrote the name *Cant*ium, and when our A.S. forefathers wrote of the *Cant*waras and their *Cant*waraburh in *Cant*land or *Cent*rice, as it still is in *Kent*. Was there an "interregnum" between A.D. 1130, under which date the A.S. Chronicle mentions *Cant*waraburuh, or A.D. 1088, where *Cent* is mentioned, and modern times when the simple (a) or (e) is alone known, in which an intrusive (u) came in, only to be thrust out again? It is not easy to believe in such vagaries in spoken language.

—*kAAnt·uaburi*: 2nd syllable. Mr. Ellis writes (er): but *·tur·* is the spelling of *E.*, *Co.* and *Ha.*, and of *Co.* in ll. 793 and 801; and *·tir·* is found in *P.*, l. 22, and *Ca.*, l. 801. These varieties of spelling surely prove an obscure sound: I confidently believe this syllable to have been sounded just as at present.

—*kAAnt·uaburi*: 3rd syllable. Again Mr. Ellis gives (be). But the word is spelt almost without exception with *u* in every MSS. in each place where it occurs: only once is it *·er·*. And this agrees with the derivation from A.S. *burh*, *burge*, *byrig*. The most probable conclusion seems to be that the origi-

ɔv iq'gelAnd tu kAAnt'ɛɹbʋri dhee wiind
dhʋ Hool'i̯ blɩs·ful maɹ·tɛɹ fɑɹ tu siik,
dhæt Hem Hæth Hɵlpen whæn dhæt dhee weɹ siik.
bɩfel· dhæt ɩn dhæt see·zun ɔn ɐ dee,

---

nal sound was (u) or (y), according to the case; but when it was possible for a careless scribe to write an *e*, this indicates just the obscure sound which the syllable now bears.

—kAAnt·ɛɹbʋri: 4th syllable. In ll. 801, 802, this word and *mury* (or *myry* or *mery*) are made to rhyme, the ictus being on the penultimate, and the rhyme a weak one. It is therefore scarcely possible to suppose the final vowel to be long.

—Hool·i̯: A.S. *hdlig*. This word in A.S. seems not to occur with *i*, but in the Orm. the vowel is long, as it is also in *prɩsstɩȝ*, *charɩȝ*, *twenntɩȝ*, *wurrþɩȝ*, &c., this last being the only word of this class that I have found at the end of a line in Chaucer, and there it rhymes with *I*. But a long syllable here so interferes with the rhythm of the verse, that it seems probable that the change of sound which the word has undoubtedly undergone was already partly effected in Chaucer's time. So probably with *sondry* (sun-dri), l. 14.

—maɹ·tɛɹ: the word is spelt *martir*, *martyr*, and *marter*, so that the variety of spelling in the second syllable seems to indicate obscurity of sound. Moreover until I am shown to be wrong in believing (iir) or (iiɹ) to be always written *ere* in Chaucer, I cannot believe the word to have ended in (iir).

18. Hɵlpen: *o* in a pure English word before *l* and another consonant, and therefore probably sounded (ɵ), as in modern English.

siik: from A.S. seóc: see §§ 106, 107.

19. Bɩfel·: the preposition *bi* or *by* (aided perhaps by the confusion which some suppose between *bi* and *ge*) bears also the form *be*, not only in Chaucer but even in A.S. In this line the Lansdowne MS. has *befel*, and in ll. 42, 52, 215, 277, 445, 572, two or more of the six MSS. have *beginne*, *besides*, *before*, &c. The conclusion is, that even though *by* was sounded like the Ger. *bei*, the vowel in compounds was often or regularly shortened. It is an obvious, but by no means a valid objection that (i) is the shortened sound not of (ɔi) but of (ii) or (ii); but as (ɔi) is a diphthong, if it is to be shortened at all, it is the latter part alone which rapid pronunciation allows to survive. Bɩfel (bɔifel·) most naturally and readily shortens into bɩfel (bɩfel·), the sound which we still use. Compare the shortening of *ou* (ɔu) first into (u) and then into (ə).

see·zun or seei·zun: the derivation of the word from the French *saison* makes it plain that the *e* is not (ii): see § 101.

see·zun: Mr. Ellis takes the second *s* as (s), the common surd sibilant. But among the multitudinous proofs of the tendency of spoken language to continue the same century after century is the rule (evidently overlooked by Mr. Ellis) given by Palsgrave for the sounding of *s*, being just the same as now holds after three centuries and a half: "If a syngle *s* come bytwene two vowelles in the meane syllables of a frenche worde by hymselfe, he shall in that place ever be sounded lyke an *z* [i.e. like an *z* ard, the old name of the letter], so that for *disant*, *paisant*, *tresor*, *rosir*, *maisôn*, they sounde *dizant*,

In Southwerk | at the Tabard as I lay 20
Redy | to wenden on my pilgrymage
To Caunterbury | with ful deuout corage
At nyght | were come | in to that hostelrye
Wel nyne and twenty in a compaignye
Of sondry folk | by aventure y-falle 25
In felaweschipe | and pilgrimes were they alle
That toward Caunterbury wolden ryde

---

faizant, trezor, rezort, maizon, and so of all suche lyke." Giles du Wes confirms this: "An *s*, in the begynnynge of a worde hath his full sounde, as dothe appere by these wordes folowyng, *sage, saunage, sapient, etc.* but in the myddes beynge eyther before a consonant or a uowell, shall be sounded lyke a *z*, as in these words *disoie, faisoie, brisoie, taisoie, etc.*" Whether the rule is the same in modern French when the *s* "in the myddes" comes before a consonant, I cannot say, as no word occurs to me in which such an *s* has not now disappeared, as in *esgard*, now *égard;* for words with *st* of Latin derivation, like *protester*, are expressly excepted by du Wes in his next rule.

—see·zun: if this word stood alone, or as a final, I hold that it would be sounded (see·zəun): see § 36. (Additional words that might have been cited in that section as representing the original French *on* by *oun* (əun) are—*bound, rebound, council, crown, ounce, pounce, count, counter* and all its compounds, *countenance, redound, roundelay, trounce* (O.Fr. *troncer*), *frounce, amount, paramount*.) But whether it would be so sounded when immediately followed by other words without any pause is obviously a different question. You rarely find in Chaucer—perhaps never, but I have not searched our seven MSS. all through with this object, though I have turned over a good many pages to see —words of French derivation in -*on* written with -*oun*, if not at the end of a line. This fact affords at least a presumption that the fuller sound was kept only where it was useful for the rhyme, but that in ordinary pronunciation these words had commenced the change they have undergone when sliding down from (əun) to (un) and thence to the present (ɐn). This shortening of (əu) into (ɐ) or (ə) we find in various English words, not only in unaccented syllables, as in New-*ton* from New-town, Ald-*us* from Ald-house; but even in spite of the accent, as when *down* gives us *Dun*-wich, *south, south*-ern, (sədh·rɐn), &c.

20. south·werk: perhaps (south·weak). *Co.* has -*work.*

—æt: A.S. not *at*, but *æt*.

—t:eb·uɹd: it is true the word comes from O. Fr. *tabar*, or It. *tabarro*, or most probably the Sp. *tabardo*, none of which have (æ); but the spelling *Tabbard* in P. shows the vowel was short, and the word is likely soon to have been completely anglicized.

21. reed·*i*: the Du. *gereed*, Ger. *bereit*, Pl. Du. *reet*, Orm. *rædig*, leave no doubt that the first vowel is long. As to the second syllable, see on *holy*, l. 17.

—wiind·en: see on *ende*, l. 15.

22. ful: the Du. *vol*, Ger. *voll*, and Orm. *full*, all indicate the short vowel, with probably the very same sound in A.S. (where the form is the same, *full*) as we give the word now.

 *i*n sɔuth·werk æt dhɐ tæb·ɹɑd æz ɔi lɛe, 20
reed·*i* tu wiind·en ɔn mɔi p*i*l·grimæædzh
tu kʌʌnt·ɐɹberi̯ w*i*dh ful de·vɔut kuræædzh·,
æt n*i*ʞht weɹ kuum *i*n tu dhæt Hɔst·elrɔi
wel nɔin and twent·*i i*n ɐ kum·penɔi
ɔv sund·r*i* fɔlk bɔi aa·ventjyyr *i*ʃʌʌl· 25
in fel·ʌshɔip, and p*i*l·grimez weɹ dh*ee* ʌʌl
dhæt tu·waɹd kʌʌnt·ɐɹberi̯ wuld·en rɔ.d.

 —devɔut·: this form can scarcely come direct from the Lat. *devotus:* the analogy of the words given in § 36—though all of these have the *ou* followed by *n*—makes it more probable that it comes from the O. Fr. *devot*, now *dévot*. Hence also there is some degree of probability that the first syllable was never pronounced (dii)—I am confident Mr. Ellis will agree with me there—but (dee) or (de̯e), and hence, when shortened through the accent falling on the last syllable, it would become (de).

 23. weɹ or wer: the final *e* was probably dropped, but its influence might still be felt in the trill of the *r*, especially before a *k* immediately following.

 —kuum : Orm. gives *cumenn*, testifying to the long vowel.

 24. wel: the Scottish pronunciation *weel* (wiil) is familiarly known, and that too is the pronunciation pointed at by Orm's spelling *wel*. But Orm also writes *well*, indicating a short vowel. And just as Orm's usage was unsettled, so in Chaucer *wel* rhymes both with (ii) words as *kele*, *whele*, *fele* (vb.), and with (e) and (ee) words as *dele* and those that end in *-elle*. The latter usage slightly predominates. Moreover in all the seven MSS. there is in this instance only one *e*, and in *Ca*. there are two *ll*s.

 —kum·penɔi: the pronunciation of the first syllable was probably with (u), as the word has that vowel occasionally in Old French; the MSS. of Chaucer sometimes so spell it; and the modern sound of (kəm) points in the same direction.

 —kum·penɔi. : *E.* and *He.* have *compaignye*, the other MSS. *companye*. In O. Fr. the forms are *cumpaignie, conpeignie, compaignie* (the most common), *conpagnie, compagnie*, &c. The old spelling might still be preserved by some scribes even when the word had assumed in this syllable the obscure sound which the variety in the spelling in our MSS. seems to point to.

 25. aa·ventjyyr·: the final *r* before a vowel following would preserve its trill.

 26. fel·ʌshɔip: in Orm. we find the termination *-shipe* always with the long vowel, as in *mannshipe*, *wurrþshipe*, &c. That it was still long in Chaucer's time is shown by the spelling in six MSS. out of the seven with a final *e*. *Ca.* alone has *-ship*. We might hope for assistance from rhymes, with *pipe*, *ripe*, &c., or with *tip*, *lip*, &c.; but no line in Chaucer, I believe, ends in *-ship*.

 27. tu·waɹd: I believe *guard* to preserve the old sound of the vowel in *ward*. In more modern times the *w* has affected the sound of *a*, making it (ʌʌ). But this was not the case in Chaucer's time: see § 76. But as the accent was apparently on the first syllable, the (waaɹd) will at least have been shortened, if it did not even lose its more distinct sound and become (wəɹd), as at present.

The chambres and the stables weren wyde
And wel we weren esed atte beste
And shortly | whan the sonne was to reste   30
So hadde I spoken | with hem everychon
That I was | of hir felaweshipe anon
And made forward | erly for to ryse
To take oure wey | ther as I yow deuyse
But nathelees | whil I haue tyme and space   35
Er that I ferther | in this tale pace

—wuld·en: if, as I have argued in § 57, the *o* in *wolde* even in A.S. was sounded (u), how comes it that the word is never written *wulde*? For *schulde* is not uncommon, like *skulda* in M.G. I suppose the reason to have been simply that in this word, as in *wolf*, *woman*, &c., our early orthographers entertained a prejudice against writing three *u*s consecutively, since they regarded the *w*, according to the name it still bears, as equivalent to *uu* or *vv*.

28. tshAAm·bɐɹz : all the MSS. in this passage have *-bres*, but in Kn. Ta. 1427 *Ca*. and *L*. have *-bere*, which *Ca*. and *P*. have in 1440. *Chamberlain* is spelt in Kn. Ta. 1418 with *bre* in *He*., *ber* in *E*. and *P*., *byr* in *Ca*., *bur* in *Co*. and *L*. For *tendre* in Prol. 150 *Ca*. has *-dere*, and *L*. *-dur*. For *engendred* in l. 4, *L*. has *-der*. For *murder* in Nun.'s Priest's Ta. *Ca*. has *-dere*, *P*. *-der*, *E*., *He*., and *Co*. have *-der*, and *Ha*. both *-dre* and *-der*, in ll. 4242, 4243, and 4247. *Shoulders* in Prol. 678 ends in *-dres* in *E*., *He*., *Co*., and *L*., in *-derys* in *Ca*., and *-ders* in *P*. In Kn. Ta. 2225 *bitter* ends in *-tre* in *E*., *He*., and *Co*., in *-tre* in *Ca*., in *-ter* in *P*., *L*., and *Ha*. Like variety is found in the spelling of other words that end in *-re* or *-er* after a consonant; and the reasonable conclusion seems to be that while the original spelling—for they all have or simulate a French origin—still has influence on the form of these words, their sound was completely anglicized and the vowel obscure; except however where the *e* was an adjective termination, and retained as such: see note on *tendre*, l. 7.

—stæːe·bɐlz : words with *-l* after a consonant show a similar (though less marked) variety of spelling to those in *-bre*, &c., just discussed.

29. eeːːed or eeiːːed : see § 101.

ːetːɐ: for (æt dhɐ), therefore both syllables sounded.

30. shAAt·lɔi: in Orm. *shorrtlike*, *shorrtli*ʒ. The rhythm, with a long syllable in the third place in the line, does not please the ear; but there are so many rhymes in Chaucer in which the adverbial *-ly* rhymes with *I*, *I* = aye, *why*, *fy*, *aspye*, &c., that it seems necessary to suppose (lɔi) to have been the usual fourteenth century pronunciation. Hart too (1569) gives *rɛrdɛi*, *sertɛnlɛi*, *uniformlɛi*, *partlei*, &c. spelt similarly to *okupːi*, *kruaifei*, &c. And Gil, as late as 1621, indicates the same sound, as I believe, in his *opnlj*, *eksidinglj*, *dɪmvrlj*, *disonestlj*, &c. See also § 16.

—wæz: A.S. *wæs*, Orm. *twass*: it is the influence of the *w* which has in course of time changed (æ) into (ʌ) in this word.

SPECIMENS. 133

dhʊ tshaamb·ɹɪz and dhʊ stæːæ·bʊlz weer·en wɔid,
and wel wi weer·en eeɹ·ed æt·ʊ best.
and shaɹt·lɔi, whæn dhʊ sun·ʊ wæz tu rest,   30
soo Hæd ɔi spook·en widh Hem ev·erɪtshoon,
dhæt ɔi wæz ɔv Hʊɹ fel·ashɔip anoon·,
and mæædˑʊ foor·waɹd eeɹ·lɔi faɹ tu rɔiz
tu tææk ɔuɹ wee dher æz ɔi jɔu devɔiz·.
but naa·dhʊlees whɔil ɔi Hæv tɔim and spæːæs,   35
eer dhæt ɔi feɹ·dhʊɹ in dhis tææl·ʊ pæːæs,

—wæz; two reasons may be assigned for believing the *s* of this word to have been (z). First, it is the old strong preterite of *wesan*, in which the *s* between two vowels was most probably (z). Secondly, it is very rare for a sharp (s) to turn into *r*, as this word forms both its 2nd singular *wére* in A.S., and its plural *wéron*: it is (z), not (s), which undergoes this change.

31. ev·erɪtshoon: on the numeral *one*, see p. 32 at bottom. All the compounds, *non, anon, echon*, &c. follow the sound of the simple word.

32. Hʊɹ: there is so much confusion of the forms *hir* and *her* in the MSS. that the words cannot have contained a *clear* sound of either *e* or *i*.

33. fooɹ·waɹd, faɹ: in Orm. the preposition *for* is always *forr*, indicating the short vowel, and there are numerous compounds all similarly spelt; but there does not seem to be a single word derived from an A.S. original in *fore-*. We must fall back therefore on the A.S. *fore-weard* as affording evidence for the length of the first syllable of this noun.

34. tæːæk: see p. 55.

—jɔu: however this may offend the 19th century ear, the pronoun *you, yow*, or *lowe*, rhymed in Chaucer with *how, now, thou*, and *prow* (= profit), *now* also once rhyming with *ynow* (= enough); and nowhere does it rhyme either with *owe, lowe, crowe, bowe, glowe, slowe, throwe, isowe, trowe, knowe, unknowe, yerowe, windowe, growe, undergrowe, Dunmowe*, nor with *schoo, do, fordo, too, therto, two*, nor again with any of the *ew* or *u* words. And as there seems to be good reason for believing *ou* or *ow* to have borne commonly in Chaucer the same sound as at present in *thou* and *now*, we accept the conclusion in the case of *you*.

35. naa·dhʊlees: see § 125.

—spæːæs: French and English tradition alike point to the certain sounding of *c* as *s* before *e, i*, and *y*, in Chaucer's time as now. This is confirmed by the derivation of *space* from *spatium*, in which there is no (k), and of *pace* from *passus*; as also by occasional varieties of spelling, as *bracer brasir, manasynge manasynge manassinge, pencel pensel, sertres certres, mynstralsye mynstralsy, encense ensense en ence*, &c.

36. feɹ·dhʊɹ: comparative of *far*, with an epenthetic *th* borrowed from *forth*; but the mollification of the vowel in the *fer* is just such as we find in the Ger. *alt, alter*.

—pæːæs: with just the sound of the modern *pass* (the same word), but prolonged.

Me thynketh it acordaunt to reson
To telle yow | al the condicion
Of ech of hem | so as it semed me
And whiche they were | and of what degree   40
And eek in what array | that they were Inne
And at a knyght | than wol I first bigynne

A knyght ther was | and that a worthy man
   That fro the tyme┘ that he first bigan
To riden out | he loued chiualrie   45
Trouthe and honour | fredom and curteisie
Ful worthy was he | in his lordes werre
And therto | hadde he riden | no man ferre
As wel in cristendom | as in Hethenesse
And euere | honoured for his worthynesse   50
¶ At Alisaundre he was | whan it was wonne
Ful ofte tyme | he hadde the bord bigonne
Abouen alle nacions in Pruce
In Lettow | hadde he reysed and in Ruce

---

37. it: when the pronoun *hit* began, as even in Chaucer's time, to lose its initial aspirate, the changed spelling indicated the loss; and no doubt if *his, her, hem,* &c. had been sounded as *is, er, em,* &c., as Mr. Ellis supposes, the MSS. would teem with evidence of the fact.

40. weer·ɛ: all the six texts omit the final *n* of this word, although a vowel follows. It is no doubt the pause that renders the hiatus tolerable; though it is conceivable that the pause itself was the substitute for a syllable here, and that the word was (weer).

42. feɪst: the variety in the spelling in the different MSS.—*first, ferst, furst*—shows the indistinct sound of the vowel.

43. man: there were in A.S., according to Bosworth, the forms *man* and *mon*, the latter of which suggests that the word might be (mɒn), like (lɒnd), (hɒnd), &c. But as it rhymes with *began*, which had only the form with *a* in A.S., we must believe the word to have been sounded with (a) or possibly (æ).

44. təim·ɛ: the A.S. would be *fram ðám tíman*; see § 126.

—hi: it seems likely that as a general rule the pronoun would be sounded long if it had the ictus, and short otherwise.

45. luuv·ed: the long vowel is proved by Orm's form *lufenn*. It is still so sounded in Norfolk. See note on (frii·dum), l. 46.

46. Honour·: the *h* may have been dropped, as undoubtedly it often was in Early French. In Mätzner's Altfr. Lieder besides the form *hounour* we have *ounour, unnour, onner, unneur*, which tell their own story. But in the MSS. of Chaucer we do not find the *h* dropped in this word or its compounds, though we do in *ostelry* (Ca., ll. 718 and 722) which we find as well as *hostelrie*, and *ost* which we have as well as *hoste*.

—frii·dum, 2nd syllable: the word is written with an *o* in all seven MSS., and therefore probably preserved the original (u) sound which we also find in

mi think·eth it acaɹdaant tu reezəun·
tu tel·ʋ jəu aal dhʋ kəndis·iəun
əv eetsh ʋv Hem, so æz it siim·ed mii,
and whitsh dhee weer·ʋ, and of whæt degrii·;   40
and iik in whæt aree· dhæt dhee wer in,
and æt ʋ kniɣht dhæn wul əi fʋrst bigin·.
ʋ kniɣht dher wæz, and dhæt ʋ wur·dhi man,
dhæt fro dhʋ təim·ʋ dhæt Hi fʋɹst bigan
tu rəid·en əut Hi luuv·ed tshiv·ʋlrəi,   45
trəuth and Honəuɹ·, frii·dum and kuɹtezəi.
ful wuɹdhi wæz Hii in Hiz lɔɔɹd·ez wer,
and dher·tuu Hæd Hi rid·en, noo man fer,
æz wel in krist·endum æz in Heedh·enes,
and evʋr Honəur·ed fər Hiz wurdh·ines.   50
æt aalisaandʋr Hi wæz whæn it wæz wun:
ful əft·ʋ təim Hi Hæd dhʋ boəɹd bigun·
abuuven aal·ʋ næsæ·siunz in pɹjyys
in let·əu Hæd Hi reez·ed and in rjyys

the Ger. *-thum*. Yet as the change towards (v) or (ə) was beginning even in Chaucer's time—see § 152, bearing in mind that the two MSS. from which I edited the *Castell off Loue* were written about 1370—the (u) was most likely already shortened. There is no such *evidence* as to *love*, though Mr. Ellis may be right in pronouncing (luv·ed).

47. loɹd·ez, 1st syllable: the A.S. *hláford* was probably nearly if not quite (hloo·vaad), with the *f* between two vowels = *v*, as also in Laȝamon, Ancren Riwle, Genesis and Exodus, Henry III.'s Proclamation, &c., we have *lauerd*, *lauerd*, *lauard*, *louerd*, *lhouerd*, and other forms, with *u*, which no doubt was the consonant. This *v* has disappeared from later forms, *lhord*, *loard*, *lord*, but when the two syllables have contracted into one, the resulting vowel is almost sure to have been long at first, and probably for a considerable period. Compare our *e'er*, *ne'er*, *o'er*.

—loɹd·ez, 2nd syllable: I have above argued, on *showres*, l. 1, that the true sound of the plural *s* is (z) not (s), relying mainly on the effect produced by the added letter or letters on the last letter of the root in certain words. A similar argument may be applied here, for though in modern English we say "my wife's brother," not "my wive's brother," Chaucer's usage seems to have been different. Turning to a few passages in The Clerk's Tale and The Merchant's Tale, I have found in the seven MSS. 49 genitives with *s* against 7 that retain the *f*. The conclusion is obvious.

48. rid·en: the infinitive is (rəid·en), the difference in the quantity of the vowel being just the same as in A.S. *rídan* and *ridēn*, or in modern English, *ride* and *ridden*.

49. krist·endum: the *i* in *christen* (verb) was short when Orm wrote, his form being *cristnenn*.

52. boəɹd: the vowel is long in Orm., *bord*, as we still sound it.

No cristen man so ofte of his degree 55
In Gernade | at the seege eek hadde he be
Of Algezir | and riden in Belmarye
At Lyeys was he | and at Satalye
Whan they were wonne | and in the grete See
At many a noble Armee | hadde he be 60
At mortal batailles | hadde he been fiftene
And foughten for oure feith at Tramyssene
In lystes thries | and ay slayn his foo
This ilke worthy knyght hadde been also
Somtyme | with the lord of Palatye 65
Agayn | another hethen in Turkye
And eueremoore | he hadde a soucreyn prys
And though þat he were worthy he was wys
And of his port | as meeke as is a mayde
He neuere yet | no vileynye ne sayde 70
In al his lyf | vn to no maner wight
He was a verray parfit gentil knyght
¶ But for to tellen yow | of his array
His hors [was] goode | but he was nat gay
Of Fustian | he wered a gypon 75
Al bismotered with his habergeon

---

57. AAl·dzheziir: the tendency to anglicize the pronunciation would cause this word to be sounded as if it were a compound of our *all* (AAl). See also note on (HAA·bɯdzhəun), l. 76.

—AAl·dzheziir: all the evidence tends to show that z in E. E. was regularly sounded as we sound it now. See for instance the note on (sæ·zun), l. 19; and, if there is independent reason to believe that our plural termination was (z), we may thence also conclude the sound of the written z from such plurals as *auez* from *ave*, which occurs frequently in Ancren Riwle. For an exceptional sound of z, see note on (servAAnts), l..101.

61. bæt·ælz: perhaps already shortened into (bæt·elz).

64. *ee*: that *aye* = ever and *aye* = yes were not sounded alike in the age of Queen Elizabeth may be shown by two arguments,—first, it is only the latter that is commonly written *I*, like the pronoun; and secondly, if they were sounded alike we should scarcely find Smith (and Gil half a century later) claiming for one of these words the same sound (Gil makes it *almost* the same —" exiguum distat"—which may mean no real difference at all) as that of the pronoun *I*, and not for the other. Chaucer's orthography agrees with tradition in sounding this adverb like the vowel of the next word, *slayn*.

66. anundh·ɯr: the frequent by-form *oother* for *other* shows that the vowel was long.

71. man·iiɹ: in the termination -*ière* in modern French the *i* is almost absorbed in the predominant *è* following. That this *i* had a much fuller and stronger sound formerly is rendered probable, independently of Chaucer's

SPECIMENS. 137

noo krist'en man soo ɔft ɔv Hiz degrii·. 55
æt guɪn·ææd æt dhv siidzh iik Hæd Hi bii
ɔv AAl·dzheziir, and rid·en in bel·mvrəi.
æt ləi·ees waɪz Hii and æt sæt·vlɔi,
whæn dhee wer wun, and in dhv greet·v sii
æt mæn·i v noo·bvl arm·ii Hæd Hi bii. 60
æt mʌɪt·ʌʌl bæt·eelz Hæd ɪii biin fift·iin,
and fɔukwht·en fɔr əuɪ feeth æt træm·isiin,
in list·ez thrəi·es and ee sleen Hiz foo.
dhis ilk·v wurdh·i knikht Hæd biin Alsoo·
sumtəiɪm·v widh dhv lɔoɪd ɔv pælvtəi· 65
ageen· anuudh·vr Heedh·en in turkəi·,
and evvrmoor· ɪii Hæd v suuv·vreen prəis.
and dhəukwh dhæt Hi weɪ wurdh·i ɪii wæz wɔiz,
and ɔv Hiz poort æz miik æz iz v meed:
Hi nev·vɪ jet noo vilenɔi· ni seed 70
in AAl Hiz lɔif untuu· noo mæn·iiɪ wikht:
Hi wæz v ver·ée paɪ·fit dzhen·til knikht.
but fʌɪ tu tel·en jəu ɔv Hiz aree,
Hiz ɪɪɔɪs waɪz guud, but Hii waɪz nɔt gee.
ɔv fust·ivn Hi weer·ed v dzhipɔun· 75
AAl bismut·vred widh Hiz HAA·bvɪdzhəun·,

---

rhymes, by Lyndesay's rhyming such words as *mateir* and *pleaseir*, for there is no evidence that the French *plaisir* (which Lyndesay's *pleaseir* is, scarcely altered) ever sounded the second syllable otherwise than with (iir).

75. *dzhipɔun·*: it may be asked why if this word was pronounced with (əun), it was not also written with *-oun*. The answer is that no educated man, such as Chaucer was, could be indifferent, if he borrowed foreign words, to the mode in which they were spelt in the language from which he took them; just as *Rome*, though it seems to have been commonly pronounced (ruum), has always been written in the manner familiar even to schoolboys as nearest to the Latin form. When such a word is used to rhyme with an English word of like sound, he might also vary the spelling, as *lamentacioun*, *toun*, Kn. Ta. 935, *doun*, *peneun*, ib. 978; but when both words are from the French, motive to change is wanting. *Ca.* however has *-oun—iojoun*, *habirioun:* in each of which words an *i* evidently stands for a *j*.

76. *bismut·vred*: the root of this word is evidently *smut*, now (smɔt).

HAA·bvɪdzhəun, 1st syllable: the spelling with *hau-* in *He.*, as in l. 2431 *hauberk* has *au* in all seven MSS., seems to indicate the sound here given. The derivation of the name of this neck-protector from *ha's* and *beorgan* accounts for this sound, the *l* having so strong a tendency to modify the (a· in the direction see § 28 of (o). We have seen a new illustration of this of late years in the constant mispronunciation of Garibaldi's name by uneducated people as (gæɪ·ɪbʌʌldɪ). But more curious it is to note that the *l* here has disappeared even in Chaucer's time (for the A.S. form was *halsbeorg*) just as

For he was late | ycome from his viage
And wente | for to doon his pilgrymage
With hym ther was his sone a yong Squier
    A louyere | and a lusty Bacheler   80
With lokkes crulle | as they were leyd in presse
Of twenty yeer of Age | he was I gesse
Of his stature | he was of euene lengthe
And wonderly delyuere | and of greet stren,;the
And he hadde been somtyme in chyuachie   85
In Flaundres | in Artoys and Pycardie
And born hym weel | as of so litel space
In hope | to stonden in his lady grace
Embrouded was he | as it were a meede
Al ful of fresshe floures | whyte and reede   90
Syngynge he was | or floytynge al the day
He was as fressh | as [is] the Monthe of May
Short was his gowne | with sleues longe and wyde
Wel koude he sitte on hors and faire ryde
He koude songes make | and wel endite   95
Iuste and eek daunce | and weel purtreye and write

---

we now always omit it in *half, calf,* &c. and *walk, talk, chalk,* &c. Compare also *bawdryk,* l. 116, from O.H.G. *balderich,* connected with *belt,* O.N. *belti,* Lat. *balteus,* &c.; and *heraudes,* l. 2599, &c., without the radical *l.*

—HAA·bœdzhəun, 2nd syllable: the various spelling with *-ber-, -bir-, -bur-,* shows an indistinct sound.

  78. went·ʋ: see note on *ende,* l. 15.

  79. suun: see below, note on l. 336.

  80. luuv·jeeɹ: the A.S. termination: see p. 67.

  —bætsh·eliiɹ: the French termination: see p. 67.

  82. jiiɹ: see p. 67.

  84. deliv·ʋr: French, but not in *-ier* or *-iere.* Cotgrave gives the form *delivre,* and according to the analogy of *chambre, tendre,* &c. (see note on l. 28), the sound will be with (ɐɐ) or before a vowel (ɐr).

  87. wiil: this form and (wel) apparently coexisted in Chaucer's English, the latter being more common. In this passage *L.* has *wele;* the other five MSS. have *wel.* See above on l. 24.

  —lai·tel: the M.G. *leitils* had apparently this sound in the first syllable. As to the quantity of the vowel in the A.S. *lytel* or *litel,* non liquet; but Orm has the forms *litell* and *litɫɫ* as well as *little* and *littɫ·ss.* In Chaucer the word is, I think, always written with one t.

  88. læed·i or læd·i: the A.S. is *hlæfdige,* to which Grein assigns the long vowel. In this he is supported by Chaucer's orthography, the word being always written with one *d,* and by the modern traditional pronunciation. Orm on the other hand has *laffdig* (vol. ii. p. 632).

fʌɹ Hi wæz lææt ɪkuum· frɔm Hɪz vɔi,æædzh·,
and went·ʊ fʌɹ tu duun Hɪz pɪl·grɪmæædzh.
wɪdh Hɪm dheɹ wæz Hɪz suun ʊ Juq skwɔi,iir·,
ʊ luuv·jeeɹ and ʊ lust·ɪ bætsh·eliɹ,   80
wɪdh lɔk·ez krul æz dhee wer leed ɪn pres:
ɔv twen·tɪ Jiɹ ʊv æædzh Hi wæz ɔi ges.
ɔv Hɪz stætJyyr· Hi wæz ʊv iiv·en leqth,
and wun·dɹɹlɔi deliv·ʊr and ɔv greet streqth;
and Hii Had biin sumtɔim· ɪn tshɪv·ʊtshɔi   85
ɪn flʌʌn·dʊrz, ɪn aʌɹ·tuɪs, and pɪk·ʊɹdɔi,
and booɹn Hɪm wiil ɹɛz ɔv soo lɔi·tel spææs,
ɪn Hoop tu stAnd·en ɪn Hɪz læædɪ grææs.
embrɔud·ed wæz Hii æz ɪt weer ʊ meed
ʌʌl ful ɔv fresh·ʊ flour·ez, whɔit and reed.   90
siq·ɪq Hi wæz ʌɹ fluɪt·ɪq ʌʌl dhʊ dee:
Hii wæz æz fresh æz iz dhʊ munth ʊv mee.
shʌɹt wæz Hɪz gɔun, wɪdh sliiv·ez lɔq and wɔid;
wel kɔud Hi sɪt ɔn HʌɹS and feer·ʊ rɔid;
Hii kɔud·ʊ sʌq·ez mæʌk and wel endɔit·,   95
dzhuust and iik dʌʌns and weel purtree· and rɔit.

---

89. embrɔud·ed: the Fr. forms have -*bro*- and -*brou*-, the modern English -*broi*-, so that we seem to be thrown back on the spelling; and *ou* in Chaucer is almost always (ou) in our traditional pronunciation.

91. fluɪt·ɪq: the derivation of Chaucer's word from the French *fluste, flute, flaute*, makes it tolerably certain that this *oy* contained an (u) sound. (Diez derives the verb *fluter* from *flatus* through a supposed *flatuer* which has then by metathesis become *flauter*. I venture to think the noun is not derived from the verb, but the verb from the noun; and that the true derivation is—still with metathesis— from *fistula*, (*filusta*), *fluste, flûte*.)

92. *E.* has 'as in the Monthe.'

93. sliiv·ez: the connexion of this word with the Fris. *slief* and Swab. *anschliefen* and *ausschliefen* (see Wedgwood), and apparently with no (e) word, seems to determine the sound.

94. feer·ʊ or feer·ʊ: *ai* commonly in Chaucer stands for (ai), but before *r* it is easier—and doubtless was easier 500 years ago also—to sound (ee). On the other hand in the West of England the sound of (ai), or nearly that, is by no means uncommon in some words. See p. 74 at top.

feer·ʊ: the final *e* is sounded to mark the adverb: see Morris, p. xlv.

96. dzhuust: from O. Fr. *juster, joster, jouster, jouster*, sounded most probably with a long vowel, which however passes through the ordinary process of shortening by the time it appears in the modern *poet's* (dzhɔstl).

97. *nikht·ʊrt·ʊrd* 2nd syll.: Mr. Ellis gives (er); but if this *uyhter*· is, as I believe, only the English form of the O. N. *natr*—noctis, pronounced nearly (naaɪt·r), it is not easy to see where the (e) comes from.

So hoote he louede | that by nyghtertale
He slepte namoore than dooth a nyghtyngale
Curteis he was | lowely | and seruysable
And carf | biforn his fader at the table   100
A Yeman hadde he | and seruantz namo
    At that tyme | for hym liste ride soo
And he was clad | in cote and hood of grene
A sheef of pecok arwes | bright and kene
Vnder his belt he bar ful thriftily   105
Wel koude he | dresse his takel yemanly
Hise arwes drouped noght with fetheres lowe

    *   *   *   *   *

Ful fetys was hir cloke | as I was war   157
Of smal coral | aboute hire Arm she bar

---

98. duuth or duth: in the Orm. the 2nd person singular of this verb had the short vowel sometimes, as *dosst* and *dost* both occur; but in the 3rd person, *doþ*, the vowel is always long. The frequency of the double *o* in the MSS. of Chaucer indicates the long vowel as still in use, whether more commonly or not is not clear.

99. kuɹtɛs': the forms *curteys*, and *courteys*, as well as the modern pronunciation of *courtesy* as (kəɹˈteɹi), combine to prove that this word, even when written with *cor-*, as in *P.* and *L.*, was not sounded with (kɔr) or (kor).

101. jiiˑmæn: Ben Jonson tells us that in his day *eo* was "found but in three words in our tongue,

        yeoman, people, jeopardy.

"Which were truer written,

        yéman, péple, jepardy."

And this *é* is elsewhere explained as the "sharp" *e*, which again he explains to mean "as in the French *i*." But the pronunciation of *yeoman* seems to have been unsettled in Chaucer's time (therefore probably in Ben Jonson's also) for some of the MSS. have *yoman* and in l. 106 *yomanly*.

—servAAntsˈ: in *E.* and *He.* the word is written with *-tz*; but in early English the *z* must have had the sharp sound of *s* when it followed a *t*, for the simple reason that the combination (tz) is unpronounceable. Occasionally the *z* was used for the two letters, being then sounded no doubt like the German *z*; as in *Le Morte Arthur*, ed. Furnivall from Harl. MS. 2252, *porz* somewhere occurs (I cannot now find it) where the *z* is evidently = *ts*, and must have been so sounded.

—nɐmœˑ: the word is *namo* in *E.*, *He.* and *Co.*, *na mo* in *P.*, *nomee* in *Ha.*, *no moo* in *Ca.* and *L.* I conclude that the long *no* (nɔˑo) had become short and indistinct, much as the same word in its fuller form *non* or *noon* (nɔˑn) is now cut short into (nən).

104. sheef: later *sheaf*, see § 84.
    — peeˈcok: later *peacock*, see § 84.
105. baɹɹ or baɹɹ: see on waar, l. 157.

soo Hoot Hi luuv·ed dhæt bɔi ni*k*ht·e*ɹ*tæɹel
Hi slept·e namoor· dhɑ·n duuth e ni*k*ht·iqgæel.
kuɹtees· Hi wæz, loou·lɔi and seɹvisæe·b·el,
and kaaɹv bifooɹn Hiz fæed·er æt dhe tæeb·el.   100
e Jii·mæn Hæd Hii, and servAAnts· numoo·
æt dhæt tɔim, fAr H*i*m list·e rɔid·e soo ;
and Hii wɹez klæd in koot and Huud ev griin.
e sheef ev pee·cɔk aar-wez bri*k*ht and kiin
und·er Hiz belt Hi bæer ful thr*i*ft·*i*lɔi.   105
wel kɔud Hi dres Hiz tæe·kel Jii·mænlɔi :
H*i*z aar·wez drɔup·ed nAk*ɯ*ht with feedh·erez loou.

       *   *   *   *   *

ful feet·*i*s wɹez Hu*ɹ* klook *ɯ*z ɔi wa*ɯ* wa*ɯ*e*ɹ* :   157
ɔv smAAl kor*A*Al· abɔut Her aAɹm shi b*ɯ*e*ɹ*ɹ

---

106. tæek·el: now commonly *tackle* (tæk·l), but in nautical mouths it is *takle* (tek·l).

—jii·mænlɔi : if any proof is needed as to the sound of the initial ʒ in Early English, two or three arguments may be advanced, as below. And perhaps they are not quite unnecessary, for I have been horrified to hear even men familiar with E.E. and with E.E. MSS. read ʒe ʒiue as (zii ziv), and so on ; while in some printed books a *z* is used as a representative of this letter, as repeatedly in the Roxburghe Club *Morte Arthur*.

    a. The ʒ in some of these words is akin to German words with *j*, as ʒong, ʒer, in German *jung*, *Jahr*.

    b. None of these words have congeners beginning with *s* or *z*.

    c. Very commonly in MSS. ʒ and *y* are used interchangeably. In this passage for instance we had *yeman* and *yemanly* in E., He., P., and Ha., while Ca., Co., and L. spell the words with ʒ.

    d. And in the MS. of the Morte Arthur just alluded to (Harl. 2252) the handwriting changes at l. 1092 (of Mr. Furnivall's edition), and in the latter part of this MS., by the second scribe, the same words—such as *ʒare*, *aʒyne*—are occasionally spelt with ʒ at the beginning of words and syllables, as are elsewhere—and always in the first handwriting—spelt with *y*.

107. nɑkæht or nɔukæht : the word is still pronounced (nɑut) in some parts of England.

    feedh·erez : the *e* is long in the Ger. *Fater* and Du. *vader*, and I believe no word which in Chaucer's time was written with the simple *e* afterwards assumed *ea*, unless the vowel was long. In the Orm. all such words had the long vowel (*æst*, *græt*, *halenn*, *hæp*, *hæþenn*, *ræd*, *sæm*, *sæte*, *tæchenn*, *tæm*, *tæress* ; *ledenn*, *redeþþ*, &c.), as most of them have also in modern English.

       *   *   *   *   *

157. feet·*i*s : this word is no doubt rightly derived by Dr. Morris from the O.Fr. *faitis*.

    waɹer or waaɹ : that this word, like *bare*, has (ee) in modern English, affords a strong presumption in favour of the thinner sound.

A peire of bedes | gauded al with grene
And ther on | heng a brooch of gold ful sheene   160
On which | ther was first write a crowned   .A.
And after | Amor vincit omnia.

  * * * * *

A Frankeleyn | was in his compaignye   331
 Whit was his heed | as is a dayesye
Of his complexion | he was sangwyn
Wel loued he by the morwe a sope in wyn
To lyuen in delit was euere his wone   335
For he was | Epicurus owene sone
That heeld opinion that pleyn delit
Was verray felicitee parfit
An housholdere | and that a greet was he
Seint Julian was he in his contree   340
His breed | his Ale | was alweys after oon
A bettre envyned man | was neuere noon
With oute bake mete | was neuere his hous
Of fissh and flessh | and that so plenteuous
It snewed in his hous | of mete and drynke   345
Of alle deyntees | that men koude thynke

---

160. br**oo**tsh : all the forms given by Littré from O. Fr., Wall., Picard., Prov., Span., &c., contain *o*, and not one of them has *u* or *ou*.

—g**oo**ld : prevailing tradition gives this sound, though (guuld) seems also to have existed. Our MSS. have the word written only with *o*.

161. aa or æǣ : non liquet ; certainly not (ee) or (*œ*).

162. æft·ʋr : A.S. æfter, Orm. *affterr*.

—aam·ʌɪ or ææm·ʌɪ : non liquet. The traditional sound of *a* in Latin at Winchester College is with the full Italian (aa), all the other vowels having their common English sound : e.g., "Benedicto benedicatur," the customary grace after meat at that college, is (bened*i*k·too benedaikaat·ʋɪ). But if this tradition is genuine, it curiously preserves a vowel-system that has no long (ee) or (*œ*); for even *æ* is not so sounded. If there really was this deficiency in the series of vowels (see § 28), it seems probable that the (aa) would be made to approach the (ii) by being modified into (æææ).

  * * * * *

334. sup : the Fr. *soupe* and *souper* as well as our verb to *sup* up, point to an (u).

335. liv'en : Orm has *libbenn* which, as well as apparently his *lifepþ* and the A.S. *lybban*, testifies to the short vowel ; though we must set against these the Ger. *lëben*, the A.S. *leofað*, and Orm's *lifeþþ* and *lif·nn*.

—del·it· : Chaucer seems to use this word in two forms, sometimes making it rhyme with *white*, sometimes with works in *-ight*, of course disregarding the guttural in this termination. Unfortunately I have mislaid my references.

wuun : the Ger. *wohnen* and Orm's *wunenn* point to the long vowel.

SPECIMENS.

ʋ peer ɛv beed·ɛz gAAd·ed AAl widh griin;
and dher ɔn Heq ɛ brootsh of goold ful shiin, 160
ɔn whitsh dher wæz feɪst writ ɛ krəun·ed aa,
and æft·ɛr aam·Aɪ vinsit ɔm·nia·

    *   *   *   *   *

ʋ fraɛqk·eleen wæz in Hiz kum·pɛnəi: 331
whɔit wæz Hiz Heed æz iz ɛ dee·ɛzɔi.
ɔv Hiz kumplek·siəun Hi wæz sæqgwɔin·:
wel luuv·ed Hi bəi dhɛ mArw ɛ sup in wɔin.
tu liv·en in delɔit· wæz ev·ɛr Hiz wuun, 335
fAr Hii wæz epikJuu·rus oo·wɛnɛ suun,
dhæt Hiild opin·iəun dhæt pleen delit·
wæz veree· felis·itii paarfit·.
æn Həus·Hooldeer and dhæt ɛ greet wæz Hii:
seent dzhJuu·liæn wæz Hii in Hiz kun·trii. 340
Hiz breed, Hiz æl, wæz AAl·weez æft·ɛr oon:
ʋ bet·ɛr envɔin·ed man wæz nev·ɛr noon.
widhəut·ɛ bææk·ɛ meet wæz nev·ɛr Hiz Həus
ɔv fish and flesh; and dhæt soo plen·tivəus,
it snJuu·ed in Hiz Həus ɛv meet and driqk 345
ɔv AAl·ɛ deen·tiiz dhæt men kəud·ɛ thiqk.

---

336. epikJuu·rus: the long *u* in Latin words rhymed with our third class of *ew* words: see § 146. The short *u* I can only conjecture to be (u).

—suun: the Ger. *Sohn* and Orm's *sun* = *filius* point to the long vowel, while the Ger. *Sonne* and Orm's *sunne* (and *sūne* perhaps also) = *sol* indicate a short vowel here, notwithstanding the fact that for now at least two centuries and a half we have not distinguished these words. Gil (1621) writes them both *sun*, and Butler (1633) expressly describes them as "woords of like sound." (Index p. a.) Chaucer commonly distinguishes *sone*, *sonne*.

oo·wɛnɛ: A.S. *ágen*, see § 46.

337. Hiild: the A.S. forms of this verb that have survived seem to be *háldan* (rather than *haldan*), pret. *héld* (rather than *hêld*). Similar are the verbs *hátan*, pret. *hét*, *slǽpan*, pret. *slép*, *cnáwan*, pret. *cnéow*, &c.; in all of which the *á* = (oo) of the infinitive has become *é* = (ii) in the preterite.

338. paarfit·: in l. 422 *Ha.* has *parfight*.

340. dzhJuu·liæn: not (dzhuu·liæn) as now. See above on *Epiwurus*, l. 336. And see p. 98, foot note †, where the word *Jew*, also written *Giwe*, may be added to those quoted.

343. widhəut·ɛ bææk·ɛ: sounding the final syllable, the A.S. forms being *wiðútan* and *bacen*.

345. snJuu·ed: *blew* from *blow* and *grew* from *grow* belong to the third *ew* class, possibly therefore *snew* also as from *snow*, though the analogy is manifestly imperfect.

347. Hii: see p. 67.

After the sondry sesons | of the yeer
So chaunged he | his mete and his sopere
Ful many a fat partrich | hadde he in Muwe
And many a Breem | and many a luce in Stuwe   350
Wo was his Cook | but if his sauce were
Poynaunt | and sharpe | and redy al his geere
His table dormant in his halle alway
Stood redy couered | al the longe day
At sessions there was he lord and sire   355
Ful ofte tyme | he was knyght of the shire
An Anlaas | and a gipser al of silk
Heeng at his girdel | whit as morne Milk |
A shirreue hadde he been and [a] Countour
Was nowher | such a worthy Vauasour

* * * * *

A Somonour was ther with vs in that place
   That hadde | a fyr reed Cherubynnes face
For sauceefleem he was with eyen narwe   625
As hoot he was | and lecherous as a sparwe
With scaled browes blake and piled berd
Of his visage | children were aferd

---

348. supiir, 1st syll.: from Fr. *souper* (or *soupier*?), which with the modern (ə) of *supper* fixes the sound.

—supiir, 2nd syll.: see top of p. 68.

349 and 350. m)yy and st)yy: see § 144.

350. l)yys: a French word. Cotgrave has *lucel* and *lucet*, Palsgrave has *lus*, and Littré gives *luset* as "nom de la truite en Bretagne." See § 138.

352. puinjAAnt: *L.* has *punyant*, which together with the French form *poignant* seems to authorize the inserted (j).

354. stuud: still pronounced in the West of England with the long vowel which the spelling indicates.

—kuuv·vrd: the French *couvrir* seems to show the vowel long.

356. shair: see bottom of p. 127.

357. dzhip·siir: Fr. *gibecière*, a game-bag, in O. Fr. also *gibacièr* and *gibeciér*.

358. giɪdəl or geɪdəl: the MSS. vary, with *gir·*, *gɪr·*, and *ger·*.

* * * * *

623. sum·unəus: from *summoneo*.

—plæɛs: see p. 56 at top.

624. tshe·rjubínez: I cannot conjecture why Mr. Ellis makes the first syllable long (tshee). It is short in the Hebrew, Greek, and Latin forms, and the metre, though it places the accent here, does not lengthen the vowel.

—tshe·rubínez: the third syllable also Mr. Ellis lengthens (bíin), which the forms in earlier languages might warrant, but four out of our seven MSS. double the *n*.

625. sAAs·eileem: the by-form with *ei* quoted by Dr. Morris, *saucefleame*, and

aft·ɐɹ dhʊ sun·drɪ see·zunz ɐv dhʊ jiɹ,
soo tshAAndzh·ed Hii Hɪz meet and Hɪz supiɹ·.
ful mæn·ɪ ɐ fæt paɹtrɪtsh· Hæd Hii ɪn mjyy,
and mæn·ɪ ɐ breem and mæn·ɪ ɐ ljyys ɪn stjyy.
woo wæz Hɪz kuuk, but ɪf Hɪz sAAs·ʊ weeɹ
puɪnjAAnt· and shaaɹp, and reed·ɪ AAl Hɪz geeɹ.
Hɪz tææ·bʊl-dAɹ·mAAnt ɪn Hɪz HAAl AAlwee·
stuud reed·ɪ kuuv·ɐɹd AAl dhʊ lɔq·ɐ deɪ.
æt ses·ɪɔunz, dher wæz Hi looɹd and sɪɹɹ:
ful ɔft·ɐ tɔim Hi wæz knɪkht ɐv dhʊ shɔiɹ.
æn æn·lææs and ɐ dzhɪp·siir AAl ɐv sɪlk
Hiiq æt Hɪz gɪr·dʊl whɔit æz mAɹn·ʊ mɪlk.
ɐ shɪr·iiv Hæd Hi biin and [ɐ] kɔunt·ɔuɹ:
wæz noo·wheer sutsh a wur·dhi væv·ɐsɔuɹ.

350

355

*   *   *   *   *

ɐ sum·ɐnɔuɹ wæz dher wɪdh us ɪn dhæt plææs,
dhæt Hæd ɐ fɔir-reed tshe·rjubɪnez fææs;
fAɹ sAAs·ʊfleem Hi wæz wɪdh ɵi·en naarwʊ·.
æz Hoot Hi wæz and letsh·erus æz ɐ spaar·wʊ;
wɪdh skAAl·ed brɔu·ez blææk and pɪl·ed beeɹd:
ɔv Hɪz vɪzæædzh tshɪl·dɹɹn weer afeeɹd·.

625

---

the Greek φλέγμα whence the second syllable is derived, show that (fleem),
not (fliim), is the sound.

626 hoot: (hɔt) in modern English, but the vowel was undoubtedly long
in Chaucer. The rhymes prove this (with *boot*, i.e. boat, *goot, smoot, woot =
knew, bot* = bit), and the spelling in *E., He., Co.,* and *Ha.* as *hoot*, and in *P.*
and *L.* as *hote.*

—letsh·erus, 1st syllable: most of the congeners of this word in the modern
languages have the vowel short: see Wedgwood.

—letsh·erus, 3rd syllable: if the ictus fell on the *-ous* of this word, I should
maintain that the sound is (ɔus), like *plentevous* rhyming with *hous*, l. 344;
but when it is not accented, I believe the syllable would naturally shorten into
that (us) which has formed a sort of half-way-house to the modern (ɔs). Compare note on *seson*, l. 19.

627 blææk: this word has two forms now, (blæk) and, as a proper name,
Blake (blɛɛk). Grein gives the vowel short in A.S., writing the word *blac* and
bla. But the word occurs frequently in Chaucer, and always, I believe, with
a single *k*, so that he must have regarded the vowel as long.

— pɪl·ed: *P.* and *La.* write *pilled*, obviously the same word as we have in
Gen. xxx. 37, "And Jacob took him rods of green poplar, and of the hazel
and chestnut tree, and *pilled* white strakes in them, and made the white appear
which was in the rods." This *pill* is evidently the modern *peel*. The Sumner's
beard had come off in patches. Where the word is written with only one *l*, I
take the sound to have been the same. Chaucer or his copiers often doubled
a consonant to indicate a short vowel preceding, but often neglected to do so.

L.

Ther nas quyk siluer | lytarge ne brymstoon
Boras | Ceruce | ne oille of Tartre noon   630
Ne oynement that wolde clense and byte
That hym myghte helpen | of the whelkes white
Nor of the knobbes | sittynge on his chekes
Wel loued he garleek | oynons | and eek lekes
And for to drynken strong wyn | reed as blood   635
Than wolde he speke | and crie as he were wood
And whan þat he | wel dronken hadde the wyn
Than wolde he speke no word but latyn

Thikke, l. 549, has only one *k* in *L*. *Hippes* has one *p* in six MSS. of the seven in l. 472. *Women*, Kn. Ta. 950, has one *m* in *P.*, but two in the other MSS. *Doked, riden* (part.), *sheperde, raray, aray*, are similar examples.

628 tshil·dum: the *i* is short in the Ormulum (chilldre) as in Modern English.

630 serjyys·: from Fr. *ceruse*, the sonant *s* being disregarded.

634 gaar·liik: the second syllable identical with *leek*, the whole word being equivalent to "garg-luigh, the pungent plant," (Rev. J. DAVIS, ap. Wedgwood).

—uun·junz: the Latin *unio* and our own modern pronunciation of (ɔn·jɐn).

dher næz kwik-sɪl·vɹɪ, lɪt·aaɹdzh, ni brɪmstoon·,
booræes·, serjyys·, nii uɪl ɐv taaɹ·tɛɹ noon,
nii uɪn·ɐment dhæt wuld·a kleenz and bɔit,
dhæt Hɪm mɪ*k*ht Help·en ɔv dhʊ whelk·ez whɔit,
nʌr ɔv dhʊ knub·ez sɪt·ɪq ɔn Hɪz tshiik·ez.
wel luuv·ed Hi gaaɹ·liik, uun·junz, and iik liik·ez,
and fʌɹ tu drɪqk·en strʌq wɔin, reed æz bluud:
dhæn wuld Hi speek and krɔi æz Hi wer wuud;
and when dhæt Hi wel druqk·en Hæd dhʊ wɔin,
dhæn wuld Hi speek noo wuurd but latɔin·.

630

635

---

make it tolerably clear that the old sound was with (u), though I do not see how to account for that vowel having been discarded from the modern French, which pronounces the *oi-* simply as (oo).

—uun·junz: the inserted (j) — as to which compare note on *poynaunt*, l. 352 — is demanded by the Latin original, by the French form, and by the forms in *ony-* in *Ca.*, *P.*, and *L.*

—liik·ez: see § 97.

636 speek: see §§ 97 and 104.

638 latɔin·: see end of § 18.

APPENDIX II.

It will doubtless be a convenience to many readers if, for the sake of comparison, I append a short specimen of Mr. Ellis's mode of pronouncing Shakspere, which, without further note or comment, I give overleaf.

Introduction.

Whan that *April* with his schoures swote
The drought of *March* hath *perc*ed to the rote
And bathed' ev'ry *veyn*' in swich *licour*,
Of which *vertu engend*'red' is the *flour;*　　　　　4
Whan ZEPHYRUS, eek, with his swete brethe
*Inspir*ed' hath in ev'ry holt' and hethe
The *tendre* croppes, and the yonge sonne
Hath in the Ram his halfe *cours* ironne　　　　　8
And smale foules maken *melodye*
That slepen al the night with open ye,—
So pricketh hem *natur*' in her' *corages;*
Than longen folk to goon on *pilgrymages*,　　　　　12
And *palmeer's* for to seken *strawnge* strondes
To ferne halwes couth' in sondry londes;
And *specially*ly, from ev'ry schyres ende
Of Engelond, to Cawnterbery they wende,　　　　　16
The holy blisful martyr for to seke,
That hem hath holpen whan that they wer' seke.
　　Bifel that in that *sesoun* on a day'
In Southwerk at the *Tabard* as I lay,　　　　　20
Redy to wenden on my *pilgrymage*
To Cawnterbery with ful *devout corage*,
At night was com' into that *hostelrye*
Wel nyn' and twenty in a *companye*　　　　　24
Of sondry folk', by *aventur*' ifalle
In felawschip', and *pilgrim's* wer' they alle,
That toward Cawnterbery wolden ryde.
The *chambres* and the *stabel's* weren wyde,　　　　　28
And wel we weren esed atte beste.
And schortly, whan the sonne was to reste
So hadd' I spoken with hem ev'rych oon,
That I was of her' felawschip' anoon,　　　　　32
And made foorward eerly for to ryse,
To tak' our' wey theer as I you *devyse*.
But natheles whyl's I hav' tym' and *space*,
Eer that I ferther in this tale *pace*,　　　　　36
Me thinketh it *accordaunt* to *resoun*
To tellen you al the *condicioun*
Of eech' of hem, so as it semed' me;
And which they weren, and of what *degre*,　　　　　40
And eek in what *array* that they wer' inne,
And at a knight than wol I first beginne.

SPECIMENS. 151

*I*ntroduk·s*i*uun·.

Whan dhat Aa·pr*i*il w*i*th -*i*s shuur·es swoot·e
Dhe druuk*w*ht of Martsh Hath pers·ed too dhe root·e,
And baadh·ed ev·r*ii* vain *i*n sw*i*tsh l*ii*·kuur·,
Of wh*i*tsh ver·tyy· endzhen·dred *i*s dhe fluur;   4
Whan Zef*i*rus, eek, w*i*th -*i*s sweet·e breeth·e
*I*nsp*ii*r·ed Hath *i*n ev·r*ii* Holt and Heeth·e
Dhe ten·dre krop·es, and dhe Juq·e sun·e
Hath *i*n dhe Ram -*i*s Halfe kuurs *i*run·e,   8
And smaal·e fuul·es maak·en melod*ii*·e,
Dhat sleep·en al dhe n*i*kht w*i*th oop·en *ii*·e,—
Soo pr*i*k·eth Hem naa·tyyr· *i*n Her koo·raadzh·es;
Dhan loq·en folk to goon on p*i*l·gr*i*maadzh·es,   12
And pal·meerz for to seek·en straundzh·e strond·es,
To fern·e Hal·wes kuuth *i*n sun·dr*i* lond·es;
And spes·*i*al*ii*, from ev·r*ii* sh*ii*r·es end·e
Of Eq·elond, to Kaun·terber·*ii* dhai wend·e,   16
Dhe Hoo·l*ii* bl*i*s·ful mar·t*ii*r for to seek·e,
Dhat Hem Hath Holp·en, whan dhat dhai weer seek·e.

  B*i*fel· dhat *i*n dhat see·suun· on a dai
At Suuth·werk at dhe Tab·ard· as *l*i lai,   20
Reed·*ii* to wend·en on m*i* p*i*l·gr*i*maadzh·e
To Kaun·terber·*ii* with ful devuut· koo·raadzh·e,
At n*i*kht was kuum *i*n too dhat os·telr*ii*·e
Weel n*ii*n and twen·t*ii* *i*n a kum·pan*ii*·e   24
Of sun·dr*ii* folk, b*ii* aa·ventyyr· *i*fal·e
*I*n fel·aush*ii*p, and p*i*l·gr*i*mz wer dhai al·e,
Dhat too·werd Kaun·terber·*ii* wold·en r*ii*d·e.
Dhe tshaam·berz and dhe staa·b·lz wee·ren w*ii*d·e,   28
And weel we wee·ren ees·ed at·e best·e.
And short·l*ii* whan dhe sun·e was to rest·e
Soo Had *l*i spook·en w*i*th -em ev·r*i*tsh oon,
Dhat *l*i was of -er fel·aush*ii*p anoon,   32
And maad·e foor·ward eer·l*ii* for to r*ii*s·e,
To taak uur wai dheer as *l*i Juu dev*ii*s·e.
But naa·dheles, wh*ii*ls *l*i -aav t*ii*m and spaas·e,
Eer dhat *l*i ferdh·er *i*n dh*i*s taa·le paas·e,   36
Meth*i*qk·eth *i*t ak·ord·aunt· to ree·suun·
To tel·en Juu al dhe kond*i*s·*i*uun·
Of eetsh of Hem, soo as *i*t seem·ed mee,
And wh*i*tsh dhai wee·ren, and of what dee·gree·,   40
And eek *i*n what arai· dhat dhai wer *i*n·e
And at a kn*i*kht dhan wol *l*i first beg*i*n·e.

KEY TO PALÆOTYPE.

a Ital. m*a*tto, Fr. ch*a*tte (mat'to, shat)
a Ger. m*a*nn (m*a*n)
ᴀ E. w*a*nt, wh*a*t, *a*ugust' (wᴀnt, whᴀt, ᴀgəst')
aa*E. f*a*ther, Ital. m*a*no (faadh'ɹ, maa'no)
ᴀᴀ E. *a*wed (ᴀᴀd)
æ E. m*a*n, c*a*t, s*a*d (mæn, kæt, sæd)
ææ Prov. E. B*a*th (Bææth)
ai E. *ay*e, Ger. h*ai*n, (ai, Hain)
au Ger. h*au*s, (Haus)

dh E. *th*ee (dhii)
dzh E. *judg*ing (dzhədzh·iq)

e E. m*e*t, G. f*e*tt (met, fet)
e E. *ae*rial, Fr. *ét*é (eiir·iɛl, ete)
ə E. b*u*t (bət)
ɛ E. r*ea*l, m*e*ntion (rii·ɛl, men·shʊn)
ee E. m*a*re (meeɹ)
œ E. *ai*ling (*œ*·liq)
əi usual E. *ey*e, t*i*me (əi, təim)
eu Ital. *E*uropa, Cockney t*ow*n (euroo·pa, teun)
əu usual E. h*ou*se (Həus)

ɪɪ E. *h*e (ɪɪii)

i E. *e*vent, Fr. f*i*ni (ivent', fini)
i E. r*i*ver, f*i*nn*y* (riv·ɹ, fini)
ii E. *e*ve (iiv)
ii E. happ*y*......(нæp·ii) in singing
iu†E. f*u*tility (fiutil·iti)
iuu†E. f*u*tile (fiuu·til)

j E. *y*et, Ger. *j*a (jet, jaa)
*k*h Ger. sie*ch* (sziikh)
k*w*h Ger. au*ch* (aukwh)

o Ital. *o* aperto, Fr. h*o*mme (om)
o E. *o*mit (omit')
ɔ E. *o*n, *o*dd (ɔn, ɔd)
œ Fr. j*eu*ne (zhœn)
oo Ital. u*o*mo (uoo·mo)
oo E. h*o*me (нoom)
œœ Fr. j*eû*ne (zhœœn)
oou usual E. kn*ow* (noou)

q E. si*n*ger, li*n*ger (siq·ɹ, liq·gɹ)

r E. *r*ay (rææ)
ɹ E. pe*r*vert, ai*r* (pəvɹt', eeɹ)

th E. *th*in (thin)
tsh E. *ch*est, ma*tch* (tshest, mætsh)

u Fr. p*ou*le (pul)
u E. p*u*ll (pul): not distinguished from (u) in this book
uu E. p*oo*l (puul)

w E. *w*itch (witsh)
wh E. *wh*ich (whitsh)

y Fr. h*u*tte, Ger. l*ü*cke (yt, lykˑe)
yy Fr. fl*û*te, G. gem*ü*th (flyyt, gəmyyt)

z E. *z*eal, mi*s*er (ziil, məi·zɹ)
zh E. vi*s*ion, Fr. *j*eu (vizh·ʊn, zhœœ)

* The double vowel indicates everywhere the same sound as the single vowel, but prolonged. The dot, as in (mat·to, ᴀgəst'), follows the accented syllable.
† I have commonly used (ju) or (juu); see note (†), p. 58.